THE NEW ENGLISHWOMAN'S GARDEN

THE NEW ENGLISHWOMAN'S GARDEN

Edited by
Alvilde Lees-Milne and Rosemary Verey

Foreword by Hardy Amies

Drawings by Louis Mackay

Chatto & Windus
LONDON

First published in 1987 by
Chatto & Windus Ltd
30 Bedford Square
London WC1B 3RP

British Library Cataloguing in Publication Data

The New Englishwoman's Garden.
1. Flower gardening—England   2. Women gardeners—England
I. Verey, Rosemary   II. Lees-Milne, Alvilde
635.9'0942   SB406

ISBN 0-7011-3273-6

PHOTOGRAPHIC ACKNOWLEDGEMENTS

Jerry Harpur photographed the gardens belonging to Priscilla, Lady Bacon;
Mrs Sarah Bott; Mrs Jill Cowley; Mrs Peter Liechti; Lady Anne Rasch;
the Hon. Miriam Rothschild; the Hon. Mrs Charles Smith-Ryland; Mrs Anne Stevens.
Muriel Hodgeman photographed Miss Anne Dexter's garden.
Andrew Lawson photographed Mrs Thomas Gibson's garden.
Tania Midgley photographed the gardens belonging to the Lady FitzWalter;
the Lady Margaret Fortescue; Miss Joan Loraine; Mrs John Makepeace;
Mrs Pamela Milburne; the Hon. Mrs Michael Payne; Mrs Joyce Robinson.
Cressida Pemberton-Pigott photographed the gardens belonging to Mrs Basil
Barlow; Mrs Nancy Boydell; the Marchioness of Cholmondeley; Mrs Sean Cooper;
Mrs M. St J. V. Gibbs; Mrs James Lees-Milne; Mrs Rupert Lycett Green;
Mrs Bryce McCosh; Mrs Reginald Sheffield; Mrs Beresford Worswick.
George Wright photographed Mrs E. N. Pumphrey's garden.
Pictures number 12 and 15 were taken by the garden owners.

Typesetting by Rowland Phototypesetting Ltd, Bury St Edmunds, Suffolk
Colour origination by Waterden Reproductions Ltd, London
Printed in Great Britain by
The Roundwood Press, Kineton, Warwick

Contents

Foreword   *page* 7

Mrs Rupert Lycett Green, BLACKLANDS HOUSE, CALNE, WILTSHIRE   8

The Hon. Miriam Rothschild, ASHTON WOLD, PETERBOROUGH, NORTHAMPTONSHIRE   14

The Hon. Mrs Michael Payne, SCOTLANDS FARM, WARGRAVE, BERKSHIRE   18

Lady Anne Rasch, HEALE HOUSE, WOODFORD, SALISBURY, WILTSHIRE   25

Mrs Nancy Boydell, THE GARDEN HOUSE, HAYTON HOUSE, ABERFORD, YORKSHIRE   30

Mrs Peter Liechti, CAMPDEN COTTAGE, CHESHAM BOIS, BUCKINGHAMSHIRE   34

Mrs Pamela Milburne, WEEKS FARM, EGERTON, ASHFORD, KENT   38

Mrs Beresford Worswick, FOSCOTE STABLES, GRITTLETON, WILTSHIRE   42

Mrs Bryce McCosh, DALEMAIN, PENRITH, CUMBRIA   46

The Marchioness of Cholmondeley, CHOLMONDELEY CASTLE, MALPAS, CHESHIRE   52

Mrs Jill Cowley, PARK FARM, GREAT WALTHAM, ESSEX   58

The Lady Margaret Fortescue, CASTLE HILL, BARNSTAPLE, DEVON   62

Mrs E. N. Pumphrey, GREATHAM MILL, LISS, HAMPSHIRE   66

Mrs Reginald Sheffield, SUTTON PARK, SUTTON-ON-THE-FOREST, YORKSHIRE   70

Mrs Basil Barlow, STANCOMBE PARK, DURSLEY, GLOUCESTERSHIRE   74

Mrs James Lees-Milne, ESSEX HOUSE, BADMINTON, AVON   80

Mrs Sean Cooper, THOMPSON'S HILL, SHERSTON, WILTSHIRE   86

Priscilla, Lady Bacon, RAVENINGHAM HALL, NORWICH, NORFOLK   90

The Hon. Mrs Charles Smith-Ryland, SHERBOURNE PARK, WARWICK, WARWICKSHIRE   96

Mrs Thomas Gibson, WESTWELL MANOR, BURFORD, OXFORDSHIRE   100

Mrs Anne Stevens, IVY COTTAGE, ANSTY, DORSET   106

Mrs Joyce Robinson, DENMANS, FONTWELL, SUSSEX   110

Mrs John Makepeace, PARNHAM HOUSE, BEAMINSTER, DORSET   116

Mrs Anne Dexter, BEECH CROFT ROAD, OXFORD, OXFORDSHIRE   122

Miss Joan Loraine, GREENCOMBE, PORLOCK, SOMERSET   126

The Lady FitzWalter, GOODNESTONE PARK, CANTERBURY, KENT 130

Mrs Sarah Bott, BENINGTON, THE LORDSHIP, STEVENAGE, HERTFORDSHIRE 136

Mrs M. St J. V. Gibbs, EWEN MANOR, CIRENCESTER, GLOUCESTERSHIRE 142

Index of plants 147

Foreword

Alvilde and Rosemary have been at it again, to everybody's delight. They have coaxed twenty-eight more ladies into writing thoughtful and informative articles about their gardens. Ray Desmond's *Bibliography of British Gardens* tells me that articles have appeared already on fifteen of these gardens. That makes thirteen newcomers. None has been described before with love, as they all are here by their owners.

Love threads its way throughout. Love of the colour, shape and smell of flowers; love of the structure of shrubs and trees, and love of the very forces of nature and of their control and fashioning into the garden.

Seven gardeners discuss their parks: 'My son and daughter-in-law have recently made a ha-ha between the lawn and the park', or 'Beyond the terrace, sunset skies are frequently an artist's dream, reflecting magical lights in the river where it was dammed in the eighteenth century to form a little lake in the park.' And there is a little tumbril talk: 'I have only two gardeners'; 'The first thing was to restore and rebuild the Triumphal Arch.' Reference is made to the planting of some seventy trees given by friends to celebrate twenty-five years of married bliss.

This unselfconscious application of the standards of the past gives the whole book great charm. Lady Anne Rasch tells us how to bring an Edwardian Japanese garden up-to-date and hits the nail of today on the head: 'This year we have started a small plant centre.'

Mrs Charles Smith-Ryland starts with 'There was little or no garden, just thirty-two rose beds,' but ends 'The old kitchen garden is now filled with greenhouses and here the talented Rodney Dedey propagates and sells shrubs from the garden'.

All is not so grand. Mrs Frances Pumphrey claims 'What I set out to do thirty years ago (and am still doing) was to create a "cottage" garden'. Mrs Anne Stevens writes: 'When I moved to Ivy Cottage in 1964 I knew it was just the type of garden I had dreamed of.' Mrs Basil Barlow admits, 'I enjoy a good dig.'

My admiration goes out to all the contributors for their enthusiasm, knowledge and taste. To Mrs Peter Leichti I bow, for starting from scratch ('I was no gardener'). Having been bitten by the bug, she got down to basics: 'My husband packed me off to Flatford Mill Fields Study Centre to take a garden botany course.' My heart warms to Mrs Sarah Bott: 'I am slowly establishing the gentle wild daffys from Cornwall which are so much more attractive than the modern hybrids.' I am delighted with Alvilde Lees-Milne for saying, 'I also think that in a small garden a certain amount of formality is necessary', as I am with Mrs Beresford Worswick for wanting 'a certain amount of formality to merge with the unruly'.

I feel quite unworthy of the task of writing this preface, yet I have read all the articles with ease. This has made me feel like a headmistress correcting essays. So full marks to everybody for taste. This book is a welcome counterweight to the ghastly lack of taste on the television. Beautiful gardens are often shown (Mrs Peter Leichti admits that hers was), but their layout and even the lie of the land are rarely discussed, and the speakers give the impression that they are not interested in garden design or its history.

I admire Mrs Thomas Gibson's garden at Westwell. She has appreciated the beauty of an existing layout, restored and enhanced it; but especial praise for her beautiful kitchen garden which is a joy to visit and, I am sure, to harvest. Hers is of the Edith Wharton orderliness sought by Rosemary Verey, Alvilde Lees-Milne and Mrs Worswick. But I must also confess to being enchanted by the true artist's dottiness of Miriam Rothschild; 'Gentians stuffed into one of those black-brown tea pots are electrifying.'

Miss Loraine must have the last word: 'Surely, behind every English woman's garden, there must be a sound and willing English man.'

Hardy Amies

Mrs Rupert Lycett Green's garden, CALNE, WILTSHIRE

When I take first-timers round the garden they fall into three categories. There are those who go round chattering about something else completely, and pass each specially prepared view with unseeing eyes, even walking over a brand new bridge without so much as a 'My, oh my!' They are the ones who take gardens for granted. That was me before I came to this. Next, there are the recently converted enthusiasts, who never stop asking questions and telling you about their own gardening problems – 'How exactly do you grow begonias from seed?' and 'When are you meant to prune ceanothus?' As I don't know the answers to any of these questions, the journey round the garden becomes fraught as opposed to serene. The last category are the old hands, who walk round in virtual silence. When they pass an evidently glorious display of tulips, they do not say, 'What wonderful tulips,' but 'What are you going to follow those tulips with?' Then, when walking round the carefully contrived vegetable garden, they say, 'If you want to see a *really* beautiful vegetable garden, then you ought to go and look at Rosemary Verey's.' They go on to describe the wonders of her garden while walking past all the things you were so desperately hoping they would praise. In the end, much the best visitors are the ones who take gardens for granted, children particularly, because they never spot the bindweed in the honeysuckle.

To begin with I knew nothing about gardening. Now I know slightly less. Twelve years ago we came here, having looked on to nothing but a pocket hand-

kerchief in London where 'Iceberg' roses remained unpruned and the odd geranium bloomed. Suddenly we owned five acres of forgotten garden. It appeared romantic enough at the time, with its lichen- and ivy-covered walls and its clouds of delicate ground elder flowers lacing old orchards. There was an air of vanished splendour about the place. It had seen its zenith in the 1880s, when seven gardeners combed its every corner; from then onwards it had been let down gently until, save for one border, all had been left to nature. This hardly mattered, for the chief magic here lies in the river, the great wide water meadow and the Marlborough Downs rising beyond.

Vaguely in this order, here's how we went. We felled 240 thirty-foot saplings which had grown around and up into the lower branches of the garden's crowning glory, a cedar 120 feet high. We hired dredging equipment and used friends to help us clear a little of the river, which was choked with silt. Meanwhile the garden was growing up fast. Rupert went to Devizes and bought a 1936 mower called Dennis, which had served a long and useful life at a distant village cricket club. Nothing much had been asked of Dennis save to mow a level pitch. Confronted with our garden, it broke down immediately. (Years later and with daintier conditions, it is now the best mower in the world.)

I became desperate and put out a cry for help. A librarian from Hay-on-Wye answered and spent the next two months hacking his way through a field of marshy bogland in the height of summer. We thought that, once cut, these willow herbs and thistles as high as us would never return. They came up again immediately, and it was only with the autumn and the return of the librarian to his books

1 The so-called herbaceous border with the seventeenth-century stables in the background. Even if there were just nettles here, it would still look beautiful.

2

3

4

5

that we saw the light. We then decided on drastic action. Dave Naish and his digger dredged the river, chucked the silt on the bog and covered the whole thing with top soil. It took a day. Rupert then spent a month laying drains, harrowing by horse and finally seeding what was to be a championship croquet lawn. Ten years later, the lawn undulates with the subsidence of the drains and the grass seed has become creeping buttercups. We still play croquet there, though.

We then took the vegetable gardens by the horns; I now realised its quality of crumbling romance could not be suspended in time indefinitely – walls were already tumbling. We sold a David Hockney drawing of me (looking surly), closed our eyes, and there was a tennis court. Simon Verity, the sculptor, carved a plaque beside it which reads COURT, COURTESY, D. HOCKNEY. That solved the problem of what to do with a quarter of the space, but there were still large areas of brambles, diseased fruit trees and ground elder.

I panicked. I decided that the only answer was to get advice from an expert. I rang up Robin Lane-Fox – I didn't know him, only his writing – and said 'Please would you come and give me some advice on the garden?' Looking back on it, it was like ringing up Yves Saint Laurent and saying, 'Please would you come and give me some advice on my wardrobe?' Robin came. He walked through the house, saw the river and said, 'Push it out into the meadow, it is much too near the house.' Even to 'Capability' Brown,

2 The new bridge, whose basic engineering was designed by Sir Martin Beckett, FRIBA, and whose top was copied from a scrumpled up photograph in *House and Garden*. We call it the Boy Scouts' hut, but the local newspaper has described it as 'The Italian Bridge'.

3 The recently resurrected grotto was probably designed by Josiah Lane of Tisbury, a famous local grotto designer of the mid eighteenth century. In describing the place, Pevsner said of Blacklands 'Not much of a house but a wonderful grotto, sadly left to disrepair.'

4 This is called the Poker Walk, lined with espalier apples bought with the winnings from a seven card high-low hand, and planted much too close together. The balls of box took three years to grow from slips.

5 One of the vegetable plots divided up by chocolate bar bricks from the stables and, when they ran out, finished off with Bradstone. Only two of the four standard gooseberries remain in the diamonds. Apples have replaced the dead.

6

7

8

6 This is the central walk down the vegetable garden chock-a-block with spring flowers and apple blossom. In the summer it becomes a solid tunnel of 'New Dawn' roses.

7 This is my favourite view of the garden. The combination of brick, clunch and ivy is completely satisfying. The path leads through arches of medlar bent into shape by Rupert. In the distance is the garden's crowning glory, a 120ft. cedar of Lebanon.

8 The site of a collapsed greenhouse is used for storing cats and bedding plants.

backed by his most illustrious client, this would have been a large undertaking. Mr Lane-Fox next spied some flagstones we were in the middle of laying in what we thought a suitable place. 'Quite right,' he said (I breathed a sigh of relief), 'Take them up, they look awful there.' As he left, he leaned from his car window and pointed out how daft the grass circle was at the entrance front of the house. 'For carriages,' he said. 'You dropped your passenger and took the carriage round to the stables. No need for that now. Anyway, what on earth has a grass circle to do with a square house?' So we made a square gravel patch for cars, laid a lawn directly in front of the house and they have given satisfaction ever since. Thank you Mr Lane-Fox.

I realized then that, unless you are suitably thick-skinned or happen to hit on a hero like Robin in a magnanimous mood, you should always pay for professional help. So along came Charlotte Evans from Hillier's. She wrote a list of mysterious names, and on Christmas Eve 1974 a lorry arrived containing 279 shrubs and plants. I had no option but to plant them instantly, since we were leaving the country on Boxing Day. I recognised the roses and very little else. I shall never forget Miss Evans' face when she inspected the gardens three years later.

In the end I am an architect *manqué* and not a gardener. I like creating instant effects and use plants for their architectural qualities and colour rather than for their horticultural interest. I am also a plagiarist; much of this garden has been copied from or strongly influenced by other people's gardens. Tulips, narcissi, polyanthuses and grape hyacinths were my mum's favourites and are mine; an abundance of artichokes and Scotch thistles are copied from John and Myfanwy Piper's Oxfordshire garden; mown paths through the cow parsley are copied from Billa Harrod's rectory garden in Norfolk; and my greatest inspiration, the idea of placing statues in unexpected places, is copied from the garden of Faringdon House (in so-called 'Oxfordshire').

There are certain facts about this garden, though, which have been inspirational from the outset. Firstly, we were bringing to life what had once been a glorious garden; discovering paths under undergrowth and blocked waterfalls. This instant archaeology was compelling. Secondly, the firm boundaries of walls, river and ha-ha made life much easier. Thirdly, anything we have built (if that is the right word) has been constructed of stuff lying around and has thus dictated itself. The waterfall bridge, for instance, is made from bits of wood from a collapsed greenhouse. The vegetable paths are made of stable bricks which were lying about in the yard, the mid-border summerhouse from Edwardian panelling removed from the house. Fences and arches are made from our own saplings, and indigenous plants such as brunnera and Welsh poppies have been spread all over the shop. Any extras have been paid for by lucky breaks. The York paving was the result of an each way bet on Pipedreamer at Ascot. The espalier apple trees were a win on a good poker hand and the gigantic urns only cost a fiver at a hotel in Torquay (they cost £100 to transport). The garden seats were swops for some very ugly tables.

Each year we usually carry out a fairly ambitious project – last year Richard Sweet, Terry Goodship, Geoffrey Nunn, a dumper truck and I (bossing about) resurrected an eighteenth-century grotto from a pile of rubble. We also built what turned out to be an extremely ambitious bridge, copied from a small and crumpled picture in a magazine, and using pieces of the recently razed Harris's sausage factory. The latest project has been a new garden in a boring and windy corner known as The Cumberland Gap. It is really an extension of the room where I sit, and will eventually sport four large topiary Indian gods in memory of my mum and two topiary Spitfires in memory of a close friend, Patrick Lindsay.

I like laughs in a garden amidst the sylvan serenity. 'Bring back the birch' is carved on a piece of slate resting against a birch stump. I like garden centre ornaments – small crocodiles, cats, doves and gnomes – placed where you might be likely to see them in reality. Because Rupert is brilliant at all games, I like each bit of garden to lend itself to some sport. The new garden is for clock golf, the lower lawn is a permanent football pitch, and the top lawn is used as an obstacle course most of the summer. To say that this is *my* garden is completely untrue. I just happen to be the manager. It could never have come about without Kenneth Cranham who built a bridge, Stuart Taylor who built many a wall and laid many a path, David Vicary who is forever pruning roses, children who are forever mowing lawns, Rupert who turns his hand to all the most difficult and painstaking work, Keith Haines who worked here as gardener for the first four years, and his uncle, Stan Chivers, who has worked harder than anyone for the last eight.

Candida Lycett Green

The Hon. Miriam Rothschild's garden,
PETERBOROUGH, NORTHAMPTONSHIRE

There are certain scenes – like certain expressions on people's faces – which become part of your life, and when you suddenly catch sight of them you relive the past and experience once again the emotions you had, strangely enough, quite forgotten. One such moment occurred when I discovered the great beauty of flowering branches of Norway maple – leafless of course, at that moment in time – seen against a white wall. It was the first week of April and I could not resist an act of mild vandalism when I came across a fairly young tree on the edge of the wood, alight with a mass of bright green flowers, spreading panicles at the end of bare branches. I took a few home and, suddenly, a room was transformed. The flowers seemed to incorporate the pale April sunlight and threw fragile shadows against the white wall. Through the window I could see thrusts of snowdrops among dry brown leaves.

This episode altered my approach to flowers in the home. Up to that time they had been, for me, still life pictures, and I arranged them like a misty Odilon Redon bouquet, or a rush of stark Dufy arums, or a vase of iris kept until they faded into Anna Tichos' tender, poetic vision of over-ness.

It is a fact that very few painters consider flowers as part of the room. They almost invariably focus on the blooms themselves, arranged in a graceful vase, or rioting forth from an elaborate marble cornucopia, or as a botanical portrait drawn on vellum, or a floral design wreathing the Virgin Mary. But the Norway maple changed all this for me. I stopped thinking of

9 Moondaisies and self-sown wild valerian grow along the edges of the path. Buddleja and 'Iceberg' roses frame the window.

cut flowers as a Dutch still life, adorned with gilded butterflies, or as a parsimonious Japanese brush drawing; from then onwards I arranged them *for the room* and its link with the garden beyond the window. Especially the open window.

If you can't paint – which is very frustrating for a gardener – you have to create your own pictures, and fortunately the seasons see to it that you have a chance to view them again next year.

My sitting-room windows are divided from the outside world by fine metal curtains, with links about six inches apart. I have found that they provide an ideal and most unobtrusive trellis for *Ipomoea* 'Heavenly Blue'. From a fair-sized earthenware pot in the corner of the window-sill, the plants romp up the sides of the curtains and soon smother them with their brilliant cerulean flowers. The great attraction of this arrangement is that both the flowers and their leaves are seen against the light – the windows face south – so that, before noon, the room is filled with a shadowy blue and emerald essence. I make a point of growing pale mauve clematis (several species, some early and some late) up the outside wall of the house and alongside the windows. I have a weakness for a juxtaposition of blue and mauve flowers. On the lawn below the window there is a mixture of purple crocus and early chionodoxa and, later, the two are linked by the fringe of cornflowers and mauve corn cockles along the edge of the gravel path. I once tried growing 'Nelly Moser' up the metal curtains, mixed with the ipomoea, but the room began to look vaguely like a conservatory – which is something I avoid at all cost.

I am passionately fond of roses and, *if* I have a

10

favourite flower, at this moment, in mid-winter, it is the dog rose, which is a blissfully untidy plant.

Roses are the flowers *par excellence* for the library. I see to it that various old-fashioned varieties like 'William Allen Richardson' and 'Golden Dawn' scramble all over the outside of the house and blur the outline of every window frame, but there is something deeply moving about a bowl of full-blown roses against a background of books ranged on tall shelves – especially the drooping lemon-yellow ones like 'Maréchal Niel', which enhances every binding, from leather tooled in gold to battered French paperbacks.

In the kitchen garden, flanked by blackberries growing on wire frames and nectarines trained along a wall, I have planted a 100-yard strip of roses, two deep, which are grown purely for use as cut flowers – with a thought for the books as the ultimate backcloth. For one all too brief period in midsummer, I can fill a bowl with 'Etoile de Hollande', adding a few 'Admiral Rodney' to *épater la bourgeoisie*. Then, suddenly, the atmosphere of the library changes, the shelves recede and attention is focused on the table and one of the great creative triumphs of man – the most beautifully shaped, coloured and scented flower in the world, and the great love of every right-minded beetle. Why is it that the nectar and perfume of roses say nothing to butterflies, yet I share with beetles this insatiable love?

Once in a while during the summer – rather late in the day – 'Stirling Silver' and 'Blue Moon' decide, after all, to produce a few flowers. The scent of these roses is indescribably sweet and melancholy. They are destined for a cut glass vase on the library mantelpiece, set against the pale, 'limed' oak panelling. I find 'Blue Moon' unreasonably, irritatingly sparse with her flowers – a nervous rose whose smoky reticence makes her the ideal companion for the thin, erudite books of reference which flank the fireplace.

My family are resigned to the fact that, as time passes, I become less and less attracted by conventional gardening. The fields edge nearer and nearer to the house. One of the links are the wild roses which grow along the terrace walls and even mingle with the cultivated varieties climbing about the house itself. Guests, on driving into the courtyard, look at the tangle of unkempt plants and wonder uneasily if they

11

10 View from one of the windows in May. The cowslips will be succeeded by a great mixture of wild flowers.

11 Poppies, wild barley, corn cockles and cornflowers combine to bring the flowers and colours of the fields indoors.

have come to the right address. Can anyone really *live* here? I have discovered that a great many plants, reaching for the light, will scale the walls. Good old *Buddleja davidii* waves its flowers over the first floor balcony fifteen feet from the ground. Sweet peas, broom, ivy, roses, clematis, Virginia creeper, old man's beard, cherry, Japanese quince, wisteria, laburnum and lilac compete for wall space.

For better or for worse, you spend quite a large slice of your time in the kitchen. This room is also protected with a thin metal curtain. Here the scarlet runner bean takes the place of ipomoea and whisks towards the ceiling like a firework. This plant, when first introduced to the UK, came as a decorative flower, not a vegetable, but in this role it has been sadly neglected. In the kitchen all depends on the receptacle you choose for your flowers. Gentians stuffed into one of those black-brown teapots are electrifying, and willow catkins in a copper kettle in the window bring April along with the scones and fresh cream.

As the fields edge forward, I have become a bulb-and-grass gardener. I think all I want is a flowering hayfield, rich in fritillaria, merging into a medieval Botticelli or pre-Raphaelite lawn, covered with all the starry, low-growing flowers, from dim violets to buttercups and daisies. The wave must stop at the foot of the stonework and lead, with a riot of climbing roses, to the sophisticated hot- and cold-house plants looking out of the window. I almost achieve this towards the end of the summer. For then, I grow the arable weeds along the narrow strip of 'no-man's land' between the grass and gravel path. They can't compete with the flora of a hayfield, but I can promote a border of poppies, perennial flax, cornflowers, corn marigolds and corn cockles and some of the less aggressive grasses. Old man's beard festoons the dining-room window, framing the gloriosa within.

I have a few plants of the original *G. rothschildiana*, which has a much tougher petal, with a stouter crinkly, yellow edge, than the species called by that name sold today. It is a wonderfully easy flower to arrange in a vase, for the plant is so subtly photopositive that the flowers all shift themselves to the outside of the bouquet to look like candles placed on a Christmas tree. It is one of those lilies which opens backwards; the petals first lie flat and then lash towards the rear, like the ears of a vicious horse. The way flowers open never ceases to surprise me. Most astonishing of all are the flannel flowers (hoya) which snap open from a central point like a whirl of clockwork toys, while

12 Waterlilies catching the light at an open window.

the yellow oxalis is rolled up neatly like a furled umbrella. I marvel too at the petals of the field poppies which, instead of being carefully layered inside the calyx, are crushed together, a bundle of crumpled red rags which don't unfold but are shaken out, never quite losing their creases.

We should be deeply grateful to Claude Monet for immortalizing that field of poppies (and the parasol!), flowers which are now being bulldozed and weed killer-ed out of our lives. For that reason, if for no other, we need them now along the gravel path. At times, who can resist grabbing a white enamel bucket and sneaking Monet's field into the sitting room, with poppies and wild barley predominating? And then you keep adding. First the cockle, then quaking grass, and Yorkshire fog; then one cornflower and another. Then you put the bucket in the empty fireplace . . .

The contrast between the cornfields' idle weeds and the hayfield flowers, which are miniscule stars in a green firmament, ebbing towards the stone walls, and the carefully and skillfully grown velvety rose and silver lily – taking over the room, books and all – engenders a strange emotion. Vague, evocative, slightly melancholy – something you hanker after, without really knowing why. But strangely enough – almost perversely – the most beautiful picture I have ever seen, successfully linking the garden and the house, is Bonnard's Open Window. You look out of this shady room to the hushed timelessness of the blazing summer sunlight. High noon. There are no flowers in the garden. Trees. The vastest breathers of the air.

Miriam Rothschild

The Hon. Mrs Michael Payne's garden,
WARGRAVE, BERKSHIRE

We saw this place properly, for the first time, early one morning in 1976 and had bought it by noon. Not bad going for someone who usually takes ages making decisions. We had lived in a larger house in the same village and, although we had always known about this house (originally a seventeenth-century chalk and flint barn and two small cottages), we had only seen occasional glimpses when driving past.

It was the garden which beguiled us. Not only did it have the same trees as we'd already planted in our own garden, but these were older and better. The mature yew hedges were smaller but healthier and easier to maintain. There was some topiary, which I loved, more rough grass and less lawn to mow. The garden was higher up, on two different levels; and it had a small wood and boggy area leading to a tiny pond, with a definite trickle of water that looked promising.

On the minus side, it was bigger and more exposed. The soil was sand in one part, heavy clay in another, and there were far too many hedges, including miles of *Lonicera nitida*. (We have got rid of a lot of it since, but what is left needs cutting at least four times a year, is extremely time-consuming and so still under the death sentence.) The kitchen garden was too big, and when we moved in six months later everything was weed-bound. The shrubs seemed to be growing in a hayfield, four sink gardens had no plants at all and that terrible popping weed was everywhere.

The real garden was on the west side of the house and drive only, with kitchen garden and courtyard to north and south. It had all been planted since 1946,

13 The swimming pool with an eighteenth-century statue of a drummer boy and surrounded by a yew hedge.

except for an old apple tree just outside the house, which provides welcome shade on the hottest days; climbing through it is Rose 'Sanders White', whose white flowers happily coincide with the pale green apples. The yew hedges in the middle of the lawn enclosed a rose garden with herbaceous borders on either side. A shrub border led to a grass circle under some lime trees, along a mown path, past a *Cedrus atlantica glauca* and *C. deodara*, around a trio of copper beech, then back through a grove of birch, amelanchiers and *Magnolia kobus* – underplanted with large clumps of daffodils and narcissi – and ended up at the house again. On the east side, four large *Chamaecyparis lawsoniana* 'Ellwoodii' guarded the front door, a clump of rhododendrons half hiding a greenhouse and, beyond that, a Scots pine, willows, two metasequoias, *Taxodium distichum* and pampas grass. Behind was a largish area of squelchy bog with oaks, several birch, a holly, ash trees and lots more willows and nuts, finally merging into woodland.

To begin with, we had enough to get on with near the house. We looked at it all with new love and excitement but also with some apprehension – so much to be done and only us and one morning's help per week to do it. Our hearts had sunk when our predecessor had said airily, 'What this place needs is a full-time gardener,' knowing only too well that he was someone probably we would never have. The first thing we did was cut the kitchen garden in half and put that down to grass, and we took away a large section of mixed hedge along the drive. A post-and-rail fence was put up to enclose the birch trees and make that part of the garden seem smaller. At least some sheep

14

could look after the rough grass instead of us.

One herbaceous border was reduced in size and the contents replanted close together to save staking. Bedding was out; silver and greys went in. Peonies were infilled with tulips planted really deep – they stay there all year long and are never taken up – and around the edge *Geranium wallichianum* 'Buxton's Variety' and *Alchemilla mollis* provide the third succession of colour.

A straggly rose bed was removed and paved with York stone; a lead statue of a drummer boy stands there instead. He looks very well in front of the dark yew hedge, flanked by two mounds of grey *Santolina chamaecyparissus*, and is the focal point of the view from our main windows. We both feel that architectural ornaments are as vital to a garden as the plants. Views and vistas are equally important and, if something is to be sited near the house, it should be planned from the house. I always consider contrasting foliage, scent and autumn colour, as well as the actual flower, when choosing new shrubs, and believe that deciduous areas should always have some evergreens and dark areas some lighter coloured leaves if possible. Thus, we replaced the dead elms (when, almost overnight, we found ourselves completely open to the outside world) with a mixture of box, laurustinus, elaeagnus, prunus and, at the far end, particularly with yew – a suggestion made by John Codrington, to enhance the white trunks of the silver birch. They were planted, for shelter, in a wavy line, leaving bays in front to be filled in later with flowering shrubs for summer interest and leaf contrast. Many more, smaller bulbs have also been put in near the daffodils to give an earlier and longer succession of blooms: snowdrops, aconites, scillas, *Anemone blanda* – not to mention hundreds of crocus, which, sadly, have failed. Every year they are cropped to ground level by rabbits, mice, deer or

15

14 Tulips, pansies, wallflowers and forget-me-nots fill stone urns in a corner of the courtyard.

15 *Chamaecyparis* 'Elwoodii' stand guard by the chalk and flint walls of the original barn.

16 The pond, with summer house based on a design by Humphrey Repton. In the bed at the water's edge are astilbes, primulas and *Ligularia dentata* 'Desdemona', with *Hosta sieboldii* behind.

17 The pond in autumn, with a large clump of pampas grass in front of a Scots fir and swamp cypress, *Taxodium distichum*, just beginning to colour.

16

17

squirrels and, much as I love our wildlife, when they are munching all my hard work, which I have waited so long to see, I confess I do feel slightly differently towards them.

All this planting, which I admit I can't resist – especially when I see ravishing things in other people's gardens which we haven't got and I long to have – has led to furious arguments. I firmly believe that more planting, particularly in corners, steep banks and awkward places which are difficult to keep, saves work. My husband is just as convinced it makes work. I say weeding needn't be done every week – mowing and tractoring does. So he is always cutting down on my planting and I am always trying to reduce his mowing. As a result of these disagreements and of always being greeted by, 'Good God – not more plants', each time I returned home with some exciting shopping or even gifts from friends, I finally resorted to hiding everything under rugs or plastic bags or locking them in the boot of the car and only getting them out late at night, hoping they wouldn't be noticed until they were safely tucked into their new home. Since so much of the garden has been planted in this way, it should really be called a Midnight Garden – not because it looks better then (although I'm sure it does), but because that is how most plants arrived here!

During all this time, we were looking out over our little valley and talking about the pond we wanted so much. We'd had some advice from professionals, but their final comment was always, 'We can't guarantee it won't leak.' Finally we decided to have a test hole dug. The solid clay underneath reassured us that it should be safe; actually seeing the trees and sky reflected in that puddle made us realise we had to go ahead. 'You don't have to mow water,' we said, so it couldn't possibly make more work. How wrong we were.

Not that the water was any trouble once it was established, but what went in and around it was. Although far less *Elodea canadensis* was put in for aeration than was recommended, it grew to such a degree that barrowloads are pulled out every year, and we are finally considering chemical action to get rid of it. Then, in order to see our new creation from the house, half the loathsome lonicera was pulled out, which meant the greenhouse, in full view, had to go too. Then the grass had to be mown after all, because it looked so much nicer. Also, I just had to have some planting at the edge – I promised not too much and at the far side only, leaving the other side plain so that we could see the surface with all its different reflections.

But the plants chosen were new to me and, in my hurry and enthusiasm for results, I stuck them in too quickly without regard for their needs. I thought just being near water would be all right – but evidently not. The edge was far too wet and sticky in winter but bone dry in summer, and the unthinkable happened: I had to water them. What lessons one learns. So the primulas, astilbes, hostas, peltiphyllum, ferns and rodgersias came out; new beds were dug lower down; the clay was exchanged for good soil compost and peat, and the plants were replaced. The gunnera has never looked back and, with its gigantic leaves, dominates the water's edge.

I had started planting some shrubs at the far end of the pond – a mixture of sun lovers, with hydrangeas and fuchsias at either side leading on to the woodland behind. Delighted as we were with all this, something was needed in the centre – some eye-catching folly perhaps. Eventually we found a pedimented rustic summerhouse made of pine logs and fir cones adapted from a Humphry Repton sketch. Now, six years later, with the trees standing tall around the edge, the planting maturing, the golden orfe sunning themselves just under the surface, the moorhens scuttling for cover and the occasional duck flying in and out, the pond looks as if it has always been there.

I love our emerging woodland garden. It was something I dearly wanted. With childhood memories of the west coast of Ireland, exotic plants and Latin names, I thought perhaps this could be similar, though on a smaller scale. Trees were pulled out or thinned, brambles grubbed up, bluebells and primroses appeared and two new ponds were made under the huge Scots pines.

So one thing has led to another. We have two regular days' help now, and extra in mid-season when we're overtaken by summer growth or for special schemes. The kitchen garden is being halved again, the courtyard paving needs attention some day, an oval swimming pool has replaced the Hybrid Teas. It was the right place after all: sunny and sheltered, surrounded by dark stone to match the statue and with no shiny blue tiles to distract the eye – lit up at night it looks enchanting. If we'd planned all these changes from scratch, we would have been horrified and done nothing, but, evolving gradually, they have given us the greatest pleasure and interest. Unlike cooking, which now takes a back seat, I find the garden most therapeutic. The longer I spend there the happier and better I feel.

There are still lots of things I would like – more shrub roses, various plant combinations, microclimates for special favourites. It will never end. There is always something to do or re-do, advice to be given, other gardens to visit, even more books to read. Whether weeding or pruning, digging up nettles or carting stones to fill the potholes, it is always rewarding. I just love it all. I am its most slavish slave. It is my favourite thing.

18 An *Acer palmatum* 'Atropurpureum', turning fiery red at the entrance to the woodland path, contrasts with the pale leaves of *Cornus alba* 'Elegantissima'.

Lady Anne Rasch's garden, WOODFORD, WILTSHIRE

In 1959, having spent six years overlooking Heale from the cottage where we started our married lives, we made the traumatic decision to move the few hundred yards across the river into the 'Big House'. We had no idea about gardens, having happily survived with a few tiny beds around the house in which we dabbled enthusiastically and spasmodically.

The lawns at Heale presented the greatest problem – our old Dennis mower took two days to cut them – and constituted our major attempts to maintain the garden. The beds, apart from a few peonies and some Poulsen roses, had been stocked with bedding plants. Using Graham Thomas's *The Modern Florilegium* and the Sunningdale Nurseries catalogue as our bible, ground cover seemed to be the answer to our prayers.

Surely no garden could offer more for the minimum of effort than Heale. The Hon. Louis Greville, my husband's great-uncle, bought it at the end of the last century and set about shaping the garden, helped in some parts by plans drawn for him by Harold Peto. With the garden lying on so many different levels, and bounded by running water, it has more scope than most gardeners dream of.

We adopted the principle of working outwards from the house by slow degrees, still with limited and unskilled labour. The outlook to the south seemed to need breaking up, as the drop in levels made the large expanse appear flat and uninteresting. We replaced

19 A rather mad medley of tulips planted somewhat haphazardly over several years! 'Queen of Bartigons', 'The Bishop' and 'Niphetos' are fronted by 'Sorbet', mixed by accident rather than design, due to the vagueness of my planting. The shrub on the left is a standard early Dutch honeysuckle.

the Poulsen roses with a thick hedge of Hybrid Musk roses planted in groups of three and five of each variety – 'Felicia', 'Penelope', 'Cornelia' and 'Buff Beauty' – all merging into one another to form a really thick hedge of varying heights and happily blending colours. They are enormously trouble-free and put up with the minimum of spraying and attention, and in recent years our gardener, Albert Tancock, has devised a very good system of supports to keep them in order. I have recently planted *Sedum spectabile* and *S.* 'Autumn Joy' at their feet, underplanting this with 'Apricot Beauty' tulips, and they give us one of our longest lasting rewards.

Below, on a lower level, we have a mixed shrub and herbaceous border, with quite a lot of height, so that walking along the middle path you are bordered on both sides by varying heights and uninterrupted views. I love the effect given by leaf colour – *Weigela* 'Variegata', *Cornus alba* 'Elegantissima', red *Cotinus coggygria*, *Rosa glauca* (*R. rubrifolia*) – and of course many greys – rue, artemisias, etc. – all interplanted with tulips, lilies, pinks and some bedding plants. We grow white, pink and yellow antirrhinums, a tall strain which we pinch out, to give us valuable patches of colour where tulips have been. Many self-sown plants – candytuft, valerian (mostly the white), red mountain spinach and foxgloves – grow alongside varieties of cranesbill, peonies, delphiniums, *Thalictrum* and goat's rue, giving us a varied and colourful bed for most of the summer, with enough shrubs to provide interesting shape in winter and to assist in supporting the taller plants through the summer.

Walking on through to the west, through a tiled cob wall, we have a widely planted apple orchard surrounded by more beds. The first of these is planted with early roses and lilies and herbaceous peonies. The central bed has roses and autumn colour, particularly *Euonymus alata*, which is always a delight with the bronzing leaves of shrub roses behind it. One day I hope the Virginia creeper *Parthenocissus quinquefolia* will help to enhance and prolong this effect, but as yet it is showing a maddening reluctance to emerge above the level of the lowest branches. Walking on past a lovely old mulberry planted at the beginning of the century, the long, wide, sloping bed presents a good variety of French roses. Their blue-based colours seem best grouped together and they make a fine show in early summer, helped by the lovely rose 'Constance Spry' grown over a pyramid support. The underplanting here is mainly peonies with a few Michaelmas daisies, variegated privet, dogwood and *Rhus*. This bed suffers from thin soil which drains too fast but is effective in early summer and in autumn when the colours of the peony leaves and the *Stephanandra incisa* come into their own.

Now the eye is drawn to the brilliant red painted bridge, a copy of the famous Nikko bridge, imported from Japan together with a unique and beautiful Japanese teahouse. This, with a magnificent stone temple lantern and several smaller stone lanterns, was brought over by Louis Greville in the early part of the century. With the help of Japanese craftsmen he created and laid out a Japanese garden surrounding the teahouse. After many years of total neglect due to understaffing in the wartime years and afterwards, this has altered in character and can now better be described as an English wild garden surrounding the teahouse. It retains an individual charm, with clever employment of the two streams which cross and re-cross with oriental ingenuity, providing a lovely setting for a mature and beautifully sited magnolia, acers and an immense cercidiphyllum. Here we concentrate on large plants and shrubs able to cope with the encroaching weeds – *Ligularia, Gunnera, Lysichiton americanum*, primulas and many other strong-growing ground coverers.

Great interest has been shown by Japanese visitors in the garden, and at their suggestion a fund has been started under the name of the Save the Teahouse Fund, with the idea of helping us to fund some very necessary repairs which we ourselves are finding hard to do. It is thanks to the incredible generosity of a friend from Japan that we have this year been presented with a whole new set of tatami mats. Arriving this week from Japan, they are the marvellous fresh green of new rushes; we cannot wait to lay them in the spring.

From the Japanese garden you walk through more orchard, well stocked in spring with daffodils, into the walled or tunnel garden. Paths and corridors of trained espalier apples and pears form 'tunnels' leading to the centre point of eight well-grown box balls surrounding a small lily pond encircled with cobbles. More tunnels formed with vines and roses, clematis and honeysuckle, laburnum and ivy lead round the outer beds. There is a mixture of wall fruits, roses, shrubs and bulbs, and always a good double row of sweet peas grown on single stems, as well as vegetables, asparagus and artichokes, currants and raspberries – a bit of everything for every season. The walls provide shelter for some of our more tender plants, although the frost seems to trickle over the walls in the most unexpected ways.

Leaving under a tunnel of fig, coupled with the Hybrid Perpetual rose 'George Dickson' whose velvet red blooms smell stronger and better than any other I know, you cross the drive and come towards the house on its west side, a lovely view from the gateway with eighty-year-old clipped yew hedges, now almost ten feet thick. We are hoping to have time to prune them 'cosmetically' in a drastic way before their proportions become too unmanageable.

The terrace on which you are now standing looks down on the house over a fine old copper boiler filled in summer with petunias. A wide paved path divides the lawns where there is an avenue of laburnums, and behind them banks of shrubs and trees. The terrace, paved with rough York stone, is furnished at each end with curved stone seats. Wide double borders of shrubs and herbaceous plants give height, with glimpses of the house between tall shrub roses, standard

20 The stone balustrades frame the terrace on the west side of the house. The height we felt we needed is given by rambling roses – 'Rambling Rector' and 'Wedding Day' – grown on two latticed tripods together with clematis 'Nelly Moser' and 'Spek's Yellow' roses. The pink rose in the foreground is 'Zéphirine Drouhin'.

21 The sloping bed, once one of our greatest problems with ground elder, is now well clothed with peonies and roses. Here *Paeonia* 'Sarah Bernhardt' with a never-failing pillar of 'Constance Spry' rose, for which *Rhus cotinus* is a good foil. The more distant colour is provided by a mixture of French roses – 'Cardinal de Richelieu', 'Tricolore de Flandre' and 'Charles de Mills'.

20

21

wisteria, delphiniums and *Crambe cordifolia.*

Here two lily ponds shape the terrace and clipped yew forms shelter from the south and north. The narrow beds round the balustrades make a lovely haven for small plants, with something flowering nearly every day of the year: cyclamen, fritillaries, *Iris unguicularis* (*I. stylosa*) and *I. reticulata*, autumn crocuses, tulips, grape hyacinths, snowdrops, night scented stocks and primulas. The two wide beds opposite the house are filled with our usual untidy medley, with quite a lot of height, helped by two ten-foot pyramids of trellis covered with 'Rambling Rector' and 'Wedding Day' roses and clematis 'Nelly Moser'.

All this has evolved over the last few years; until recently we have looked after it with one full-time gardener and with help with grass-cutting and major maintenance. We are well mechanised, more than half the lawns mown by gang mowers drawn by a wheel-horse tractor, our edges dealt with by an excellent machine used more often in large cemeteries. Jacob sheep help with some of the rough grass after the bulbs have played their part.

We have started a small plant centre, with the idea of being able to take on more help in the garden. I feel that, gardening on this scale, one must excuse oneself by endeavouring to make the garden self-financing. I also see a delightfully widening scope of planting; the garden in the last twenty years has been almost entirely and economically furnished by the progeny of other parts of the garden, with a resulting lack of variety in the beds. Now there is a positive need to introduce new plants and shrubs, and I am able to apply my favourite maxim, when in need of an excuse for extravagance, of 'cheaper in the end'! So I hope that we are now setting out on a new era of enhancement and improvement along the lines so beautifully laid out for us in those early years of this century.

22 A really magnificent *Magnolia* x *soulangiana* provides a marvellously oriental framework to the view of the Nikko bridge from the Japanese teahouse.

23 The rather despised *Prunus* 'Kanzan' gains distinction when seen reflected in the stream running beside the Japanese garden with a lovely long view of Wiltshire water meadows beyond.

24 The Japanese teahouse, a feature of the garden laid out by Japanese craftsmen earlier this century.

25 Here, as in so many parts of Heale garden, the 'hand of nature' has been allowed to get out of hand! *Alchemilla mollis* and sisyrinchium break any attempt at formality such a wide area of paving might suggest. The standard box bushes provide annual nesting for the blackbirds.

26 Two long borders break the flatness of the croquet lawn, the highest level being Hybrid Musk roses fronted with *Sedum spectabile*, and at a lower level a mixed shrub and herbaceous border. In the foreground is the rose 'Cornelia' with *Geranium psilostemon* rather shockingly growing into it – also giant grey thistle. Behind 'Felicia' and 'Penelope' merge into each other.

23

24

25

26

Mrs Nancy Boydell's garden, ABERFORD, YORKSHIRE

The garden at Hayton House is entirely my own creation – planned, planted and maintained by me for twenty-seven years. In the past I had remade several gardens, but here I was, at fifty, starting afresh with a third of an acre of derelict garden chock-a-block with docks, nettles and couch grass – and no help.

The farm lies in gently rolling countryside to the west of the plain of York, about 120 feet above sea level. Built from local stone, the Georgian farmhouse stands on the north side of a shallow valley, with a small walled garden in front and a triangular plot, once a kitchen garden, to the west. I was lucky, for the soil is a well-drained, friable loam. As we are in the magnesian limestone belt, it has a pH of 7, which means avoiding calcifuge plants. This did not worry me; I am no lover of rhododendrons and there are lots of good plants that will grow well in an alkaline soil.

My first job was to get rid of the weeds. The family ploughed the old kitchen garden and hopefully I planted potatoes as a cleaning crop. The weeds came up thicker than ever; in despair I watered the lot with a solution of sodium chlorate, and left it for six months to leach out. The rest of that first summer was spent digging out couch grass in the little walled garden and laying a small terrace of paving stones along the front of the house.

During the winter I read every book I could find on garden design, finally deciding on a round lawn with wide borders to the west and a path leading north to a summerhouse with a view across the valley. The site for the lawn was levelled as much as possible by raking

27 The steps leading from the rose garden are decorated with terracotta pots of pelargoniums, lobelia and the white daisies of *Chrysanthemum frutescens*.

and, with plenty of limestone around, I made shallow terraces for alpines on the remaining south-west-facing slope. All this resulted in a slipped disc, so that I spent the next two years gardening on my knees!

As my previous gardens had been well sheltered, I had never seriously considered wind damage. One hundred young plants of *Chamaecyparis lawsoniana* were carefully planted around the boundary to make a nice evergreen hedge. Come March I had a row of little brown objects, quite dead. Then it was back to the books to study wind protection. I reluctantly spent £30 on chestnut palings with rabbit netting at the base, for I had also forgotten the wildlife menace. A field away, Hayton Wood provided some shelter, but the wind whipped around the house and buildings, so that strategic plantings of tough shrubs was necessary. The handsome *Olearia macrodonta* makes a marvellous windstop on a draughty corner. *Osmanthus* x *burkwoodii* is another stalwart evergreen with scented flowers that has served me well.

I then decided on a boundary planting of mixed shrubs to the west and laurels to the south. I had yet to discover how difficult it is to keep a laurel hedge to size. Mine finished up about eight feet across the top, so that trimming it became a nightmare. The shrubs have not only provided a windbreak: various viburnums and philadelphus, *Kolkwitzia amabilis*, a golden *Cornus alba* 'Spaethii' and *Cotoneaster salicifolius* also provide flowers, foliage and berries in due season. *Syringa* x *persica* is now six feet across and, unlike the common lilac, never fails to reward me with dainty trusses of mauve scented florets in May. A 'Buff Beauty' rose now mingles with the gold of the cornus. Seeking quick results, the borders around the lawn were filled with modern roses in sunset colours, to reflect the evening sky. However, I came to dread the annual battle against thorns, and pruning and spraying every fortnight against disease is not my idea of gardening. The borders looked so dull in winter that the roses had to go.

Inspired by the writings of Margery Fish and Vita Sackville-West, I longed for beautiful perennials with evergreen basal leaves that would cover the bare soil, leaving no room for weeds. I became a member of the Northern Horticultural Society, and often visited their trial gardens at Harlow Car, near Harrogate, and the lovely gardens at Newby Hall near Ripon.

But making lists of plants is not enough. Size, hardiness, the kind of soil they like, all have to be considered. Are they sun lovers or do they need shade? Having chosen the plants, what neighbours shall we give them to show off their beauty to perfection? Learning the hard way, by trial and error, I now harden my heart and get rid of unsuitable plants. I love trying new plants, and on discovering 'silvers' I went mad, for they flourish in my warm, well-drained soil.

In the little walled garden senecios, santolinas, helichrysums, *Teucrium fruticans* and even the tender *Convolvulus cneorum* mix with pinks, lavender and rosemary against a background of escallonias, hebes and clematis. The Afghan sage, *Perovskia atriplicifolia*, persists in growing between the paving stones in spite of several applications of weed killer. It is just as well that the front door is never used, for it is almost blocked by a large *Escallonia* 'Iveyi' – a most handsome evergreen with panicles of white flowers in August.

With the borders now full, I wanted even more plants, so I was given a piece of field to the south. It was on a lower level than the rest of the plot and so out of sight in winter: I decided it was to be a summer garden, and planted shrub roses, hardy geraniums and ornamental herbs. With large spreads of lavender around the shimmering silver leaves of an *Elaeagnus commutata*, it is a riot of scent and colour in July.

I am a great believer in feeding well to prevent disease, so in March, June and July I give the whole garden a top dressing of a granular fertiliser high in potash and phosphates and low in nitrogen. Potash is marvellous for flower colour and for ripening woody stems in autumn to prevent frost damage. Everything is given a good start with a mixture of peat and John Innes compost around the roots when planting.

Seven years ago, when my husband died, we converted some outbuildings next to the house into a bungalow, so that I did not have to leave my garden. I can now step out of my window on to a small terrace, where a lovely *Rosa chinensis* 'Mutabilis' on the west wall nearby carries a succession of single roses from June to November. The pointed buds are copper-coloured, opening to pale apricot and fading to rose pink. In a corner the white flowers of *Clematis* 'Marie Boisselot' look exotic behind the shining leaves of *Fatsia japonica*.

On cold days I can enjoy the spring garden without stepping outside, for in the shade of two beautiful Japanese cherries – the white-flowered 'Tai Haku' and the creamy-yellow 'Ukon' – is my collection of hellebores, surrounded by snowdrops and aconites. The *orientalis* varieties have long-lasting flowers ranging from pale pink to wine red, with the pale yellow of *Helleborus kochii* for contrast. The green flowers of *H. corsicus* and *H.* x *sternii* are handsome for many weeks, while the 'Potter's Wheel' form of the Christmas rose, *H. niger*, has large flowers of pure white.

Dicentras, pulmonarias, bergenias, omphalodes and hepaticas also enjoy the shade, and the foliage of *Geranium macrorrhizum* and *G. phaeum* hides the fading leaves of the spring bulbs. There are a few lilies for late summer and then Japanese anemones and the hardy cyclamen take over. With the winter flowers of *Viburnum farreri* and *V.* 'Dawn', and the red berries of a cotoneaster to follow, planting takes care of itself all the year round. The only work is removing the dead leaves of the hellebores and collecting the seedlings, and keeping the anemones in check.

Most bulbs, except the woodlanders, do well in my garden. Species tulips increase rapidly. *Tulipa tarda* and *T. urumiensis* are almost a nuisance, but I forgive them in April when they make a golden circle around the millstone in the middle of the lawn, nearly smothering the alpines. Many alpines also make excellent ground cover on the rockery slopes, together with an assortment of thymes.

Clematis like an alkaline soil too. The wine-red flowers of *C. viticella* 'Rubra' mingle with the pale pink 'New Dawn' rose, while the yellow blooms and silky seed heads of *C. tibetana* ssp. *vernayi* (formerly known as *C. orientalis*) almost smother a cotoneaster for weeks. Favourites among the summer perennials are the penstemons and campanulas, violas of all kinds and *Erysimum* 'Bowles' Mauve', which is never out of bloom. It looks super with a pale yellow broom. Achilleas, peonies and irises have good leaves as well as flowers, while hostas and euphorbias are unrivalled for foliage display.

My pride and joy at the moment is my Mediterranean bank, which lies in full sun between the west garden and the summer garden. Getting rid of the laurels three years ago left me with a level border five feet wide above a gently sloping bank six feet wide, the whole forty feet long. Helped by Beth Chatto's book *The Dry Garden*, and keeping the planting low so as not to spoil the view either way, I went to town on cistus, dwarf hebes, santolinas, calaminthas, dianthus, marrubiums and thymes, resulting in a grey-green effect. Diascias and osteospermums bloom for weeks. Rosemary and a silver-leaved ozothamnus grow near the steps, where *Olearia* x *scilloniensis* is a mass of white daisies in May.

Although the garden is full, I try to give plants enough space, light and air, presenting a garden picture that is in keeping with the house. I started with an empty plot. Looking back, I can't imagine how I had the patience to wait for the young plants to mature. Although I sometimes wish for a larger garden, I know I have as much as I can manage. I keep a diary and last year worked an average of ten hours a week from March to November – there is very little winter work.

Making a garden is only a beginning; one lifetime is not enough to travel all the highways and byways into which curiosity about plants can lead. Discovering how a plant works, its native habitat and history, reading volumes of plant lore and visiting other gardens all add to the enjoyment. Above all, there is the sharing of knowledge and plants with other enthusiasts, for gardeners are a most generous species. In spite of all the ups and downs, I can happily echo John Gerard, a gardening enthusiast of a much earlier age, who – in 1697 – asked, 'Who would look dangerously up at planets, who can look safely down at plants.'

Nancy Boydell.

28

28 Alpines, bulbs, low growing perennials and dwarf shrubs provide colour and interest all through the year and are easy to maintain.

29 A corner of the rose garden in early June. 'Nevada' is in full bloom, with Clematis 'Barbara Dibley' entwined in its lower branches. *Rosa gallica* 'Complicata' is opening the first of its pink and white blooms. In front, *Geranium ibericum* makes a colourful ground cover.

29

Mrs Peter Liechti's garden,
CHESHAM BOIS, BUCKINGHAMSHIRE

In June 1968, newly married, I came to live at Campden Cottage, having resigned from my job in London and intending, I suppose, to become a non-working wife. The house was taken over immediately by builders and decorators, which made my presence indoors superfluous; knowing no one in the area, my attention focused on the garden.

If the house was in a mess, the garden was even worse. It covers half an acre and had been well laid out in the early 1920s in a style typical of that period, with straight lines and York stone paths everywhere. I was no gardener and had no particular intention of becoming one, but this little plot had received scant attention for several years. The house backs south, but all was overshadowed by too many large trees. The laurel hedge which surrounds the property was overgrown; large areas had been neglected for many years, and weeds and grass were everywhere. Clearly there was work to be done.

Fortunately I took some photographs before work started. This continued for the next few years, unfortunately not systematically and there were some gaps, particularly after June 1972 when my daughter Penny was born and I became extremely maternal, no doubt to the detriment of the garden. These early photographs are not particularly good but have proved invaluable, as I have since given numerous talks on the development of my garden.

30 A view of the garden looking south, showing mainly trees and shrubs planted within the past twelve years, including the cedar. Plants have been chosen as much for foliage as flower, and numerous herbaceous plants and bulbs help to provide interest throughout the year.

The pulling up of my first weed should be engraved on my memory, but I had no idea what a significant step this was. Previously I had never given gardening a thought and, if anyone then could have predicted the way my life was to develop, I would not have believed them. The original intention was simply to clear and tidy the garden and replant where necessary. I knew no other gardeners, and did not think to seek advice; I usually prefer to find things out for myself. Initially my husband helped at the weekends although he is not the greatest garden enthusiast; he felled four large trees that shaded the drawing room, laid part of the terrace, and claims to have dug every one of the flower beds at least once.

It took at least two years to clear the garden, the soil of which is heavy alkaline clay, and I made many mistakes. Masses of Madonna lilies, which had not flowered that first summer, were discarded through ignorance; paths were weeded by hand, thereby dislodging paving stones – for some reason I thought it was not done to use weedkillers. Even now I use them reluctantly, just on the grass and paved areas. Beds and borders are still hand weeded, which has now become necessary as they are full of plants and self-sown seedlings. Another mistake was to plant what I was assured by a nurseryman would be a dwarf cedar – a deodar – and which has to be pruned every year or it will become too dominant. However, when it was young I changed the character of this tree by removing alternate layers of branches, thus emphasising the individual tiers, with their attractive drooping ends.

During these two years it became apparent that there was nothing much worth keeping: a couple of shrubs, two round, golden yew bushes and a large, beautifully shaped weeping ash which is unfortunately positioned in the centre of the almost square back garden. It also became clear that it would be costly to restock the large beds, so I took a part-time job for two and a half years, and spent all my earnings on the garden. I joined the Royal Horticultural Society to receive its journal. Unfortunately I had no idea at that time how useful the Vincent Square shows would have been.

A neighbour remarked casually one day: 'You are ordering your trees and shrubs from Hillier's of course?' 'Of course,' I replied, not caring to admit that I had never heard of Hillier's. Throughout this period I was reading avidly and at one time had twenty-nine library tickets. I started to buy the more useful books, which led to another interest: a collection of some of the better nineteenth- and twentieth-century gardening books – which I wish there were more time to read. The most useful book at this time, given to me in 1969, was the newly published *Dictionary of Garden Plants* in colour by Roy Hay and Patrick Synge, which had colour photographs of many of the plants that I was reading about. I well remember seeing for the first time in reality a *Viburnum plicatum* 'Mariesii' and feeling the intense satisfaction of knowing what it was, and furthermore, knowing that it was not 'Lanarth'. Clearly I was falling in love with plants and could not learn enough about them, but without realising it, I was starved of gardening company. In 1974 my husband packed me off to the Flatford Mill Field Study Centre to take a garden botany course.

For some ten years I have been collecting rare and unusual plants and, with the help of friends, propagate selected subjects each year for sale for the National Gardens Scheme. As the garden is very cold, only hardy plants are grown; these have been acquired from nurseries and other gardens all over the country. They attract many visitors who appreciate the chance to see and purchase plants which are not difficult to grow, but which are not easy to obtain.

Another appealing factor is that the garden is small enough for the average gardener to relate to. The visitors know that all the work is done by one person, including cutting those vigorous laurel hedges, the only task that I dislike. Occasionally I have help with grass cutting, but only because it is time-consuming. Weeding I find positively therapeutic. There is really too much work for one person, and more time has to be spent on maintenance than one would wish, but I

enjoy the results, and so do the visitors, many of whom return frequently.

The aim is to grow nothing but the best, but I will try any promising, unfamiliar plant, except obvious lime-haters. In 1983, when the garden was about to be featured on television, the producer asked me for the names of plants that were likely to be interesting in early September. I listed more than four hundred, many of course not for their flowers but because of their shape, foliage or rarity. I grow many hybrids and cultivars, but love species plants and look forward to the time, some years ahead, when domestic commitments reduce, and botanising holidays abroad become possible.

What of the plants? There are large collections of daphnes, euphorbias, my beloved hellebores, cistuses and salvias (which do surprisingly well in spite of the climate), viburnums, shrub and species roses, including *Rosa glauca* (*R. rubrifolia*), which has become my trademark. This goes into every garden that I design, except window boxes! Dianthus abound, various forms of *Alchemilla*, epimediums, hostas, alstroemerias, agapanthus, magnolias, of which *M. kobus loebneri* 'Leonard Messel' is a great success. There are also eryngiums, some gorgeous lilac species, many charming violas, numerous peony species and cultivars, bergenia hybrids with leaves that turn red in winter, and masses of narcissi, mostly the dainty Cyclamineus hybrids. There are many clematis growing up trees, into shrubs and up walls, and several herbaceous types. There are many more shrubs and herbaceous plants, a list of which would be tedious to read. The trees include *Prunus subhirtella* 'Autumnalis Rosea', *Acer pseudoplatanus* 'Brilliantissimum', *Acer negundo* 'Flamingo', *Acer davidii* and other snake barks, *Betula utilis jacquemontii*, *Metasequoia glyptostroboides*, *Prunus serrula*, *Davidia involucrata*, in its infancy, and others besides those already mentioned. The finest plant of all is a well-shaped *Acer griseum*.

The garden to the rear of the house has been altered gradually and considerably over several years, and much has been swept away to accommodate a large York stone terrace.

The whole garden has greatly changed, although the layout of the beds and borders is based on what was here originally. It is not large but has a feeling of spaciousness, peace and tranquillity which gives me great satisfaction and which, I hope, is shared by all who come here.

31

32

33

31 Beneath the dominant spire of *Juniperus communis* 'Hibernica' is a medley of plants – acers, a magnolia, pulmonarias, epimediums and hellebores, including a fine plant of Valerie Finnis' hybrid 'Boughton Strain'.

32 Roses dominate this picture. From the right are 'Céleste', 'Pink Grootendorst', 'Climbing Cécile Brunner' and the Hybrid Musk 'Penelope'. The south-facing bed against the house contains many sun lovers including agapanthus, alstroemerias, *Romneya coulteri*, *Jasminum revolutum*, *Commelina coelestis*, cistuses, fuchsias and a fine *Abutilon* x *Suntense*.

33 Corner of a border in late Spring. A fine Canadian hybrid lilac *Syringa* x *josiflexa* 'Bellicent', as sweetly scented but more graceful than the English lilacs, stands beside a small tree, *Acer pseudoplatanus* 'Brilliantissimum'. This is well-known for the bright pink of the new leaves which mellow to pale green. Even in maturity this tree retains its umbrella shape.

Mrs Pamela Milburne's garden, EGERTON, KENT

I started gardening when I grew mustard and cress in tiny saucepans belonging to a very beautiful toy stove, one heated by methylated spirits given me by my Aunt Emily – we lived dangerously in the nursery in those days. Needless to say, I was severely reprimanded for using the wrong things for the wrong purpose – I had already given my tea set the same treatment. I have never understood why no one ever gave me a flower pot.

I have had four gardens since then, one each in Surrey and Kenya and two in Kent. Now I have landed on a patch of Wealden clay which is hard work digging and weeding but – to everyone's surprise and my delight – grows many things well.

Kenya was very exciting and experimental in 1947. We lived at 7,500 feet – high enough for Kent violets and the occasional daffodil. To my astonishment pelargoniums, or geraniums as I know them, preferred to grow up a house and seeded themselves lavishly, resulting in some lovely and interesting colour variations. My worst weed was freesia, a great improvement on my present bindweed problem.

When I returned to Britain in 1958, a good friend advised me to get a book called *The Mixed Border* by Christopher Lloyd. That really got me hooked and, one day, with my daughter, we headed for Great Dixter to have a look at his particularly beautiful border. There we were lucky enough to find the great man himself under a bush, busy weeding. Greatly daring, we interrupted his labours to tell him how lovely his garden was looking, and then started on my

problems. He was immensely kind and we went off home full of new ideas. And he made me a plan.

I was lucky enough in those days to have a gardener, so the digging was no problem – or not mine, anyway. I made the borders either side of a brick and stone path some nine feet wide – it was originally the drive, ending in iron gates. The borders are seventeen feet wide and, where they curve, wider still. I have planted everything myself and my success quite astonishes me when I look around today. I had problems with the plan: it kept on blowing away, so I often put things the wrong way round. It got very muddy too. It just goes to show that it is not too important where things are planted if they are in large enough groups – what I call swathes. They seem to join up better than blobs, and I reckon that is the reason why my borders look better from top to bottom rather than from side to side. I am also inclined to idleness and appreciate things that seed themselves and flow into each other, resulting in muddles which I prefer to describe as interesting mixtures – a point to be argued.

My best self-seeding plant is my poppy. I call it 'my poppy' because I cannot remember how it came here in the first instance. Every year the variety of colours changes – pinks, mauves, corals, single, double and very double. It shows that I do not do much digging. Phlox do very well on this heavy soil, and for many years I had a fantastic display of Madonna lilies – but botrytis dashed my conceit into the ground, aided and abetted by a cold winter and wet spring, and by my forgetting to spray in time as advised. I have not managed to get them going again in any other part of the garden, but will go on trying. One has to start again from seed to get free of botrytis, I am told, and

34 The mixed borders on either side of the old drive are filled with *Lysimachia punctata*, *Sedum* 'Autumn Joy', phlomis and delphiniums.

35

from my experience, that is true.

I had planted *Griselinia littoralis* as a background hedge to the borders, but it could not take the wet spring, which was disappointing, as it remains a lovely fresh green all the year and needs very little attention with the shears or, preferably, secateurs. Without this background, I found that I had to start off two more developments. The first was the creation of a sober pattern which I worked out from an upstairs bedroom window and, for the second, I swopped round things that were growing well and shapely and overlapping the grass edge. Cistus always grow unexpectedly here and kniphofia make enormous clumps; *Sedum* 'Autumn Joy' and the tiny little flat conifer type, whose name I never can remember, suddenly took off in every direction, really enjoying the situation. I never have the heart or, today, the strength, to move it.

In the middle of the remaining area of grass, which was very wet in winter, I put a tiny little swamp cypress, *Metasequoia* something-or-other. It has now grown into a very tall, attractive tree. Still with this and that to find a home for, I dug another bed and stuck in some willow twigs. There are so many forms of willow, and all so easy to get going. Stick it in the ground and it grows. I hope that, in due course, I will have winding grass walks with as many varieties of willow as I can collect. And I don't mean buy. It is more fun to meet up with a new type and take a tiny twig home – with permission, of course. I do not pay enough attention to names and find that labels spoil the effect.

I am delighted that I have infected my daughter with my garden addiction. She finds it very useful to prop- agate from my plants. She gardens in Cheshire, an underrated gardening county, with more clement weather than Kent, and she often replaces plants which have been unable to survive our sometimes cruel winters and wet springs, as well as finding lovely things of her own.

I enjoy seeing other gardens; my favourite, other

36

35 The oriental poppy, a wonderful self-seeder which changes colour and form each year.

36 *Papaver somniferum* and *Salvia* x *superba* against a background of pink erigeron.

37 *Papaver somniferum* or opium poppy with Scotch thistles, *Gladiolus byzantinus* and *Campanula lactiflora*.

38 *Cotinus coggygria*, *Rheum palmatum* or ornamental rhubarb and honesty in the mixed border.

37

38

than Dixter, is John Treasure's at Burford House, Tenbury Wells. It is simply lovely and he has made the whole thing himself. What a challenge – could enthusiasm make up for ignorance? I think the answer is yes, as gardeners are very kind and generous with advice, encouragement and cuttings.

I am trying to reorganise things round the pond, having cut down the last willow, which dropped all its leaves into the water and shaded it too much. 'It is quite a large pond, and I hope to get some interesting boggy plants going for the summer, with the help of Beth Chatto's book *The Wet Garden* and some grandchildren. In due course I will have an even more delectable view for breakfast, lunch and tea – weather permitting. One has to give enough time to standing and staring – sitting and eating and, let's hope, admiring. Then, wouldn't it be an improvement if . . . and there we go again!

Pamela Milbourne

Mrs Beresford Worswick's garden, GRITTLETON, WILTSHIRE

I inherited my love of gardening from my father. (He was not only a talented gardener but also something of a naturalist.)

The actual making of a garden came only when I had my own home and, several moves later, when I arrived at Foscote Stables. The garden here was started approximately fourteen years ago on a not very promising site sloping down to the north, with a variety of soils – predominantly alkaline, with some shallow and stony parts, some clay and some deep, rich and neutral soil. The whole site was bounded by dilapidated farm walls, stinging nettles and the stumps of felled trees. It was very exposed, particularly to our prevailing southwesterly wind, so our first priority was to create shelter.

To provide the quick shelter and screening that we needed so urgently, and with the help of a man for four afternoons a week, we dug trenches and planted x *Cupressocyparis leylandii*. Yew would have been nicer, but it takes too long to grow and the cattle grazing in the adjoining fields made it out of the question. The cypresses grew at least three feet a year; with hard clipping from the word go, they now make a good, neat hedge some fifteen feet high and are hardly recognisable as the sometimes rather despised *leylandii*.

The hedges provided the shelter we needed, but we also had to establish some level areas on the site, especially near the house. This is how we came to build walls and steps. The colour and texture of natural stone make a wonderful background for plants, especially when seen with the dark black-green of the hedges.

We came next to planting trees – silver birch and balsam poplar – both fairly quick to establish and the latter lovely with its delicious scent when the leaves are just breaking. Another favourite is *Prunus serrulata*, with its wonderful mahogany-coloured bark.

A few trees and shrubs have travelled with us from Sussex. One of them is *Cornus kousa*, which flowered for the first time in 1980. Another is a splendid evergreen viburnum, bought thirty-five years ago. This tree has been moved four times in its life, but the leaves are as green and glossy as ever. We planted most of the hedges and trees within the first five years. It was hard work keeping them watered in the first two summers, especially in 1978 when the use of hosepipes was forbidden. We are lucky to have two wells in a small paddock; they kept us going through the drought, though it meant moving the water by bucket and carrier for two months. It was all worthwhile – we did not lose a single tree.

I had no grand plan in mind when we started the garden; it just evolved. I like to see contrast of form, with large groups giving way to quiet little corners more intricately planted. But I am not a tidy gardener; I like a garden to be richly filled, so that the plants overflow and intermingle as naturally as possible. Shrub roses and clematis do this very well and I have used them extensively. Throughout the seasons, pots and troughs add interest and colour, filled with tulips, pansies, lilies, petunias, agapanthus and an occasional tender shrub. I do want a certain amount of formality to merge with the unruly. I am very fond of box as a

39 Looking eastwards from under the vine-covered pergola. The small, sheltered beds against the house are planted with *Convolvulus cneorum* and *Lithospermum* 'Heavenly Blue'. Against the wall is a campsis.

garden shrub and have used cones and domes of it throughout the garden – most successfully, perhaps, immediately outside the sitting-room windows.

Much of the garden is seen from these windows. The nearest lawn, which is quite small, is bordered on either side by stone walls covered with many clematis and roses. The borders are filled with favourite perennials: *Paeonia mlokosewitschii*, delphiniums, white oriental poppies, campanulas of all kinds and *Phlox paniculata*. The border on the north side is planted with early bulbs and tree peonies. Steps lead to the second lawn, which is roughly circular in shape. The east side is stony and rough but things do grow after a pickaxe has made the planting holes. Here are several trees, including gleditsia and snake bark acer. All are underplanted with crocosmia and *Euphorbia griffithii* and many other things. On the west side is a wisteria-covered pergola and, in front of this, the lovely rose 'Ispahan'.

On leaving this garden through a yew archway, we come to a larger area containing the croquet lawn. Facing south is a very successful bed planted with *Eremurus robustus* – the first to flower – followed by *Eremurus stenophyllus (E. bungei)* and lovely *Alstroemeria ligtu* hybrids, and lastly *Romneya coulteri*, which carries on until the first frosts. On the east side is a row of pleached limes, and, inside the boundary wall, wild roses, philadelphus and all kinds of bulbs – narcissus, early crocus and fritillaries. On the west side are many trees and, in one of the larger areas of neutral soil, beds of azaleas and primulas.

Beyond this a bog garden, for moisture-loving plants, leads to the duck enclosure, where two ponds were dug out with a bulldozer and puddled with clay. The banks we planted with hedgerow shrubs and trees such as wild cherry, guelder rose and spindles; it all looks quite natural and is home for many ducks – teal, tree ducks, carolinas, mandarins and pochards. Moorhens have made their home there too. The whole area has had to be wired against foxes. It looked quite hideous at first, but now the wire is hidden with shrubs and roses – anything that my cats cannot climb.

The return to the house is by a grass walk between borders of sweetly scented shrub roses backed by beech hedges. A gate leads from here into another little walled garden, featuring a beautiful standard wisteria. When planted, about twelve years ago, it was in a very sickly condition, but it grew so quickly that it has almost taken over the allotted space.

Lastly, we go down a few steps to another small

40

garden in front of the kitchen and overlooked by the conservatory, which gives us much pleasure in winter since there is always something in flower: jasmine out for Christmas, two *Rhododendron* 'Fragrantissimum', which, as the name implies, have a heavenly scent, and an abutilon which has flowered continuously for twelve months.

There is still much for me to do, and I do have regrets. Some of the plants I love, such as fritillaries, cyclamen, dogs's-tooth violets and many more, I should have planted in hundreds rather than in dozens, and why did I not plant *Cornus nuttallii* years ago? I should have been looking forward, by now, to seeing the flowers of this beautiful tree every spring. However, what is completed has grown and multiplied so much that, on Open Day, we can find many good plants for the plant stall, and it is pleasant to have a surplus of good things to give to friends, just as I have, in the past, had many lovely plants given to me.

41

42

43

40 From the small paved garden, enclosed by the yew hedge, a path leads through the Beech Walk planted with old roses, interspaced with poles for clematis and honeysuckle.

41 East side of the garden: on the wall is a *Clematis montana* and, in the foreground, white geranium with geum and late tulips; on the upper level, a snakebark acer, backed by a tall beech hedge.

42 A view looking up the garden to the circular lawn and the croquet lawn beyond. Two junipers flank the stone steps; a pair of yews, in the distance, are being trained to form an arch.

43 Looking from the bog garden to the neutral soil area, a young *Acer* 'Brilliantissimum' and *Acer griseum*, surrounded by various azaleas, primulas and bulbs of many varieties.

Mrs Bryce McCosh's garden, PENRITH, CUMBRIA

The garden at Dalemain is very old, having grown with the centuries around the tower built by the powerful de Morville family in 1156. The terrace, with its extensive herbaceous border, has developed on the western side of the tower, along the edge of a rocky limestone bank which, in earlier days, created excellent natural defences.

As more peaceable times came to Cumbria, a medieval and Tudor Manor House was added to the tower, while the garden grew from one of necessary herbs and vegetables to a place of beauty and design. An Elizabethan Knot Garden was planted with small beds, framed with sweet-smelling boxwood, reflecting the designs of plaster work decorating the ceiling in the panelled Fretwork Room. The Knot Garden, originally double its present size, is still filled with herbs and scented flowers for medicinal and culinary purposes. These, and others grown throughout the garden, are used for pot-pourri, Dalemain long having the reputation of being perfumed with herbs and beeswax.

Come with me for a meandering walk round our much-loved garden, for I love to talk about the plants and different trees that grow in this rather heavy, mainly alkaline soil. It is not easy soil, becoming what we in the north call 'clarty', though some areas are more friable thanks to generations of beech and oak leaves working their way into the rich, red earth. Trees

44 Aconites carpet The Grove from early January till the end of March, with snowdrops and periwinkles. Later, clusters of *Lilium tigrinum* arise from the woody undergrowth of tulip trees, lilacs, hollies and elms. This small wood is protected by a medieval defensive wall, partially crenellated, surrounding the courtyard. The pigeon loft dates from 1745 and is still lined with the original flagstone nesting boxes.

grow well, providing necessary shelter from harmful winds. The small wood protecting the house is carpeted first with glorious golden aconites, snowdrops, periwinkles and, later, with a sprinkling of tiger lilies. These were here long before I was born, for all my family, since they came to Dalemain in 1679, have been foresters and gardeners. This deeply inherited love of the land has been passed on to our generation and our children's also.

Among these aconites, *Liriodendron tulipifera* grow, sheltered by walls of medieval buildings in the courtyard behind the house, and another eighteenth-century tulip tree on the lawn flowers in good summers. *Magnolia wilsonii* blossoms among holly and yew near a young *Davidia involucrata*, the dove tree, while various maples provide autumn colours.

Shelter is of primary importance when planting a garden; one can get away with frost, but, in the north, we must be fully prepared for long cold winters. Frequently more tender shrubs, Japanese maples, young magnolias and so forth, have wigwams of fir branches tied securely over their forms until the beginning of June, for late frosts are a frequent hazard.

The early Georgian, classical addition to the house has balustraded, leaded roof walks which are ideal places from which to view the garden stretching up towards Friarsdarock and the Beck, where monks from Dacre's monastery fished and walked in these woodland glades. Beyond the terrace, sunset skies are frequently an artist's dream, reflecting magical lights in the river where it was dammed in the eighteenth century to form a little lake in the park.

Around pedimented windows on each side of the front door, pale pink China roses flower profusely,

45

46

reflecting sympathetically the colours of the sandstone behind. Some were planted at least eighty years ago and recorded in watercolour paintings by the family. They have limited root run, since they grow in stone wells below the level of the sandstone walk in front of the cellar windows. Every blink of sun reflects upon these walls, and yet, with infinite care, these old China roses are the first and last to bloom, even in the Christmas season. Well rotted manure in early spring, sometimes a dressing of fresh soil, and fortnightly feeds of liquid manure in the growing season keep them in good health, not forgetting regular waterings whenever needed. Among crevices, the old-fashioned yellow fumitory and an unusual breed of perennial antirrhinums seed freely.

Turn the corner, beneath an ancient yew tree, on to the terrace where rambling and climbing roses form enormous bushes growing in the gravel walk. These roses are partially pegged down in long arching sprays – 'Albertine', 'New Dawn', 'Emily Gray', 'Paul's Scarlet Climber', 'Dorothy Perkins', 'Paulii' and 'Blairii No. II'. Against the drop of the mighty wall below, eating apples growing in the Low Garden produce delicious fruit. The Low Garden was laid out as an eighteenth-century landscaped garden, bordered on the far side by the Dacre Beck, but now a meadow, it brings a feeling of peace and tranquillity to the scene.

The great herbaceous border on the terrace presents a challenge. Backed by a tremendously high curtain wall, the sun shines relentlessly on it, or winds buffet from the south-west and the Ullswater Fells. Loads of farm manure spread each winter put goodness back into soil harassed by the elements. Roses and other climbers must be watched with eagle eyes in case precious young branches come adrift and break. A

45 The terrace walk, looking towards the house, with the mighty *Abies cephalonica* planted at the west end in 1686. The sundial, made by Robert Whitehead of Kirkby Stephen in 1688, can be seen in front of the border with a glimpse of the house beyond. Hostas and earlier spring bulbs, including a very unusual snowdrop, *Galanthus nivalis* 'Miss Hasell', named and probably 'found' at Dalemain by one of my great-great aunts, grow in the foreground border.

46 The terrace walk is sheltered by Sir Edward Hasell's immensely high wall, rebuilt in 1685 by James Zwingler who specialised in building walls and staircases. The ha-ha, dropping perpendicularly into the Low Garden, is also his work. The long, wide herbaceous border has long been one of the glories of this garden, where spring flowers and bulbs grow well, followed throughout the season by perennials and climbing plants.

vast *Clematis montana rubens* climbs the wall, struggling to throw tendrils into cracks on topmost coping stones. Virginia creeper, *Hedera* 'Sulphur Heart' ('Paddy's Pride') and *H.* 'Goldheart', ruby-leaved *Vitis* 'Brandt' and jasmine have all been planted in an effort to clothe the wall further, each climber positioned to help its neighbour, for every plant needs a nurse plant to keep it in good condition.

Among all manner of herbaceous plants, including delphiniums, monkshood and cimicifuga, gentian-blue *Anchusa* 'Dropmore' makes a lovely show for many weeks. Old-fashioned rudbeckias and *Eupatorium purpureum* create a fine display until it is time to cut, fork and thoroughly clean the border for another season of spring flowers: aubrietas, pansies, forget-me-nots, and bulbs begin the calendar all over again. Tulips love the terrace; being children of the Middle East, good drainage on this border suits their needs and they multiply happily. Crocus too, both spring and autumn varieties, grow in the gravel walks and are encouraged to do so among low-growing rock plants. This is an all-the-year-round garden; there is not a single week when some plant is not in bloom, when foliage plants, shrubs or trees do not create additional beauty.

At the furthest end of the terrace, beyond the sundial dated 1688, grows a magnificent Greek fir, *Abies cephalonica*, planted about the same date by my ancestor Sir Edward Hasell. One hot autumn, cones were collected and dried and their seeds, sown in wooden boxes, were left outside to be striated by frosts. It was exciting to be able to plant young trees a few years later in both garden and neighbouring woods.

Edward Hasell employed a Mr Zwingler to build high garden walls, against which he planted apple trees and apricots, the latter brought back from London by coach on one of his many uncomfortable journeys to attend Parliament. The Zwingler family had arrived from Holland after the Restoration. James Zwingler delighted in building walls and staircases and, from the shadowed end of the terrace, a short flight of steps leads into the High Garden where his tremendously tall orchard walls provide shelter. An open summer house built into the wall contains most of its original oak seats, decorated with flowers and fruit which can still be seen beneath coatings of preservative paint. The vista from this point is like a fairy-tale, especially when morning sunshine casts magical lights upon the garden laid out below. Colourful borders, lawns, and the Knot Garden lie in the shadow of the Greek fir, with Victorian glasshouses built against the Tudor brick walls of the older part of the garden; beyond, the house and its picturesque jumble of roofs and chimneystacks and the courtyard with massive stone barns and stables.

One of the glories of the garden is the collection of shrub and old roses which have been gathered over the years. Scented Damask roses, such as 'Ispahan' and 'La Ville de Bruxelles', intermingle with Gallica beauties flowering profusely for many weeks. Species roses and thorny briars play their part. Many have histories, having been given to me by friends and relations from other gardens. The vigorous trails of *Rosa filipes* covered with myriads of yellow-centred, perfumed flowers hang over the wall among ivy, above steps leading down into the Wild Garden beside the beck. *Rosa hugonis*, an old Species rose from China, is first to bloom; this enormous shrub, covered with small, pale yellow flowers, is a never-to-be-forgotten sight. Nearby a wealth of blue Himalayan poppies bloom, *Meconopsis grandis* G.S. 600; established years ago, they grow in various places, including the rich alluvial soil of the Wild Garden. These glorious patches, like blue skies reflected upon earth, are a particular strain brought back by George Sheriff from Himalaya.

Groups of hardy agapanthus grow well, in winter time appreciating a feed of farm manure. Their large heads of blue trumpet flowers on stiff stems look exotic near the lily pool in the centre of the Knot Garden. The half-hardy variety stand outside in frost-free months.

Plants have always been my love. When I was a child I collected and pressed wild flowers or retrieved throw-outs from the rubbish heap beyond the potting shed. These were laboriously barrowed to various woodland gardens beyond the confines of the 'Grown-up garden'. Will Stuart, head gardener at Dalemain for half a century, was my true friend, and today the garden is being faithfully cared for with his watchful spirit guiding everything I do.

The garden is full of friends: pear trees given as Christmas presents grow in company with that glorious dessert apple 'Nonsuch', which Williams the Planter installed here in 1786; *Aster x frikartii* with clouds of starry flowers; lilacs; stars of Bethlehem; that glorious white-barked silver birch *Betula utilis jacquemontii* planted to celebrate our Queen's Silver Jubilee; golden elms as memorials to our fallen native trees, and many more. Wisteria rambles up Mr Zwingler's south-facing walls. *Eccremocarpus*, flame trumpet Chilean Vine, has survived two winters; fourteen degrees Fahrenheit of frost is a regular occurrence.

The Wild Garden, at the furthest end of the eighteenth-century Low Garden, becomes a carpet of wild flowers overshadowed by fruit trees. Useful herbaceous plants beside the beck give colour when spring bulbs have died down; *Macleaya cordata*, coral-coloured and stately; *Senecio macrophylla*, *S. przewalskii* and *Ligularia dentata* 'Desdemona' with golden flowers and ornamental leaves; *Euphorbia griffithii* 'Fireglow' – these grow with relatively little care. Cherries and crabs interspersed with spire-like junipers line paths, while variegated hollies and *Rubus x tridel* 'Benenden', with glistening white flowers on arching branches, overlook a little cemetery below the wooded bank, where some of the many dogs we have all loved are buried. *Meconopsis grandis* flowers among fragrant *Azalea pontica*, while many late varieties of narcissi and bluebells hold their own.

The vegetable garden, not to be forgotten, is an early cultivated area against high walls of the Deer Park. Peepholes were built within its frame where fallow deer, grazing quietly, could be spied and shot. Alongside vegetables and sweet peas, cuttings of many sorts are hopefully, and usually successfully, rooted, while in a shaded corner beside a holly hedge, Christmas roses and Parma violets multiply.

Dalemain can proudly sport a flower for every season of the year, whether it be sweet-scented *Viburnum farreri* in winter, or Rose 'Céleste's' perfect pink buds and flowers in summer time. It truly is a much loved garden.

Sylvia Mary McCosh

47 Eighteenth-century summer house built into the wall of the High Garden. Shrub and species roses have been collected over the years; one of these, 'Madame Lauriol de Barny', a mid nineteenth-century Bourbon, is shown in full bloom.

48 The Elizabethan Knot Garden in Spring, when tulips provide rich colour, their bulbs remaining to multiply beneath carpets of perennial herbs. In the background, Barton Fell and Swarth Fell rise to summits where Roman Legions marched.

49 The Knot Garden filled with sweet-smelling herbs including both mauve and white *Viola cornuta*. Golden marjoram creates a foil surrounding fuchsias, lilies, silver artemisias and southernwood in the central beds. Beneath spreading branches of ancient yews, a panorama of the Ullswater fells is seen beyond rolling parkland.

50

47

48

49

The Marchioness of Cholmondeley's garden,
MALPAS, CHESHIRE

It seems to me that there are three types of gardener: the plantsman, the garden designer and the fortunate gardener who combines both qualities. I find I am the middle one, the rarity of the plant taking second place to its effect on the picture. I am not really a plantsman. Certain plants I love more than others – most especially the dwarf bulbs – but my love is shared by so many other garden dwellers. And their love, alas, is gastronomic!

In the same way the gardens I read about seem to fall into three categories: the garden that is created from scratch (such was my mother's garden in Norfolk, created from a stubble field in the 1920s); the already well-established garden; and then a mixture of the two, the inherited garden, with established bones and framework but no planting as such, just waiting like a pen and ink outline to be filled in with shape and colour.

Our garden at Cholmondeley was the latter type. Shape, flowing contours, trees, great masses of shelter, paths, water – all the framework, but no infill. I think, in a way, that this is the most satisfying of all, presenting the opportunity for creative work, but with the background already there.

The original Cholmondeley Hall had stood on the same site from very early days, the private chapel alongside dating from 1285. In 1801, the 1st Marquess decided to build a castle on the nearby Fir Hill.

50 A view over the Temple Garden. Evergreen Azalea 'Eddy' flowers by the waterfall, which drops about 10 feet over sandstone rocks and pools, through the rock garden and into the pool via the Dolphin Bridge where a galaxy of Koi carp hover to be fed. The temple can be seen on the first island.

Much of the structure from the Old Hall was used for this, including very fine ironwork by Tijou and Bakewell, some of which went into the garden. He left the walled kitchen garden *in situ* by the chapel and, until the last war, this continued to supply the castle with fruit, vegetables and flowers, which were taken up the hill, daily, in a wheelbarrow.

I longed for a flower garden and particularly for flowers to pick for the house. I had been brought up in gardens of which flowers and scent, the formality of paved paths and walls, terraces, clipped hedges and stone urns formed an integral part, and, nostalgically, I longed to create something similar. But to have converted our grassy slopes would have meant much structural work, not to be contemplated where long overdue estate work was priority number one.

The existing rhododendrons, laurels and May trees reminded me of hated walks in the London parks as a child, so my eventual commitment to developing and creating a garden of substance and beauty was slow to take off. Also the whole area was overrun with rabbits, and anything we planted was immediately ravaged.

We fenced in an area, the size of two tennis courts, and made a double herbaceous border and a rose garden. It took me hours to design the rose garden, but the planning and the result filled me with such pleasure and such a sense of achievement that, from then on, I was bitten by the gardening bug. It bit slowly to begin with and, with no trained head gardener, I made all the inevitable mistakes, in spite of the fact that I read every gardening article I could find. Few, if any, of the garden books that I pored over ever counted on their readers having to start from a weed-infested jungle. I

51

was fortunate in having parents whose encouragement was really the driving force at the beginning.

We have at Cholmondeley the sort of soil my father had always longed for – acid and loamy. He introduced me to some of those great gardens in the south, where began my love affair with magnolias, and to Bodnant, whose beauty took my breath away. There I discovered the extent and excitement of the rhododendron and azalea world. The late Lord Aberconway gave me my first precious rhododendrons, Elizabeth and *augustinii*.

I realised in the early days that there was no time to be lost where 'the giants' were concerned, and the varieties of magnolia, acer and camellia, and the davidia and many others which I planted then are now mature trees and form the background to all the later planting. Unfortunately I did not think sufficiently 'big' in those days, and the early plantings were very meagre.

Like so many other gardens, the droughts of 1976 and 1977 caused casualties among these early plantings and encouraged honey fungus. I lost my favourite magnolia – the only *M. salicifolia* in the garden – this way. It was very beautiful. It seemed always to be covered with myriad white butterflies every April. It flowered at the same time as the enormously tall old

geans and, with a carpet of cream and white daffodils, against the background of the white wrought-iron gates by Bakewell which span the drive, was a ravishing symphony in cream and white every spring.

Over the years, we engaged the services of several professional gardeners, particularly in the Temple Garden which was then, and still is, the show piece – a beautifully laid out water garden lying hidden at the bottom of the long grass slope and surrounded by trees and great haystacks of hybrid rhododendrons. The water area is big enough to hold two small islands, upon one of which stands the small four-columned temple after which the garden is named. In the early days the water was muddy and overgrown by yellow water lilies. After three bulldozers had cleaned it out and it had been filled with sweet clean water, the gardener and I spent a whole day rowing round the islands dropping hundreds of plastic baskets containing water lilies and oxygenating plants into its watery depths. And what a sight they are now in the summer.

The view from the top of the rockery, which drops down into the Temple Garden, is very beautiful. One glimpses the waters of Moss Mere out in the park beyond, between two groups of slim cupressus. This rockery originally looked very Victorian, and the

54

sandstone rocks stood out of the soil like almonds in a fruit cake. So we employed the late Brian McKenna (a great expert on Snowdonia), who completely relaid it, using some of the carved sandstone capitals – scattered relics of the Old Hall – as steps. He also constructed a natural-looking waterfall, which is now fed by a newly directed, little winding stream.

The chief influence in our early planting was Jim Russell, a great visionary planner, and under his direction many hundreds of rhododendrons and azaleas were planted, as well as trees in the park. He also altered the shape of the double herbaceous borders, filling them with the Hybrid Musk roses 'Prosperity', 'Felicia', 'Cornelia' and 'Buff Beauty', and the lovely modern shrub rose 'Fritz Nobis', planted among groups of geranium, astrantia, *Campanula lactiflora* and many other herbaceous plants. A real stroke of genius was to place two full standard *Pyrus salicifolia* 'Pendula' in each bed. Their height – approximately twelve feet and still growing – brings the herbaceous area into proportion with the size of the garden and the surrounding trees.

My original rose garden remains the same. The eight L-shaped and the two rectangular beds are raised, in a paved area, and there are four double arches to give height. These were covered with climbing roses, but they were badly damaged in the winter of 1982 and I have had to replace them. Meanwhile, until these new climbers gain height, the arches are covered in mid-summer with the sweet-scented old-fashioned sweet peas, and a cobaea or two to give height. On a warm evening in high summer the scent is quite wonderful. Roses are not really happy in our light acid soil, so we need to change them, and also the soil, periodically, and have to feed them lavishly. They are mostly Flori-bunda, with four standard 'Ballerina' on either side of the paved path.

The castle stands beautifully and imposingly on the hill, but much planting on the surrounding terrace would have been incongruous. It needs the expanse of grass flowing on down to the park and the garden area below. But we did plant some big, evergreen shrubs such as camellias and mahonias and the more

51 Small pool at the bottom of the Temple Garden. The stone heron, holding a fish aloft, came from my grandmother's garden in Stagglethorpe Old Hall in Lincolnshire.

52 Waterlilies just starting into flower in the Temple Garden pool.

53

54

statuesque climbers like *Magnolia grandiflora* and *Hydrangea petiolaris* on and around the building – their height and proportions complement the great sandstone blocks of the castle.

Initially all our early clearing and planting was at the bottom of the slope and among the trees where the ponticums and laurels gave shelter, but I soon discovered, looking out of my bedroom window on a cold morning, that the frost tended to lie in this low area, and it cleared more quickly further up the slope towards the castle. I now plant all the more tender climbers and shrubs at the bottom of the terrace wall just below the castle. Here I grow *Abutilon* x *suntense*, *Daphne odora*, *Carpenteria californica*, *Ceanothus* 'Trewithen Blue' and several hebes.

In 1967, I was able to indulge my taste for designing when we opened up a fairly big area on the south side of the castle, cutting through the terrace to show the previously hidden lower windows of the building. A swimming pool and sandstone loggia in the Gothic style flank this sunken garden on one side, and a small silver-planted garden, leading up to the castle by two levels of stone steps, on the other. We used some of the beautiful Bakewell iron railings from the Old Hall both here on the steps and in the loggia.

Since opening to the public in 1976, we have had money to spend on machinery and new projects, and now we employ more gardeners. In 1972 we reclaimed some of the park area in which to plant some seventy specimen trees given to us for our twenty-fifth wedding anniversary by many of our friends – a charming idea and much to be recommended. The most recent project has been to clear and plant up part of the woodland area of Tower Hill behind the castle. Sadly a lot of beautiful old beeches had to come down. They were a hazard, and it was too risky to leave them, but we do miss them. The Countryside Commission gave us a grant and arranged the replanting of indigenous trees in this area. With the help and advice of Vernon Russell-Smith, we underplanted with several groups of rhododendrons, azaleas, eucryphias, *Pieris formosa forrestii*, camellias and magnolias.

There is a tremendous future for this woodland area, and I was encouraged to find during the long hard winter of 1985/6 that the lower walk in Tower Hill (which is still underdeveloped) appears to have been less affected by the frost than the rest of the woodland area. Everywhere else in the garden was rock hard and very sad-looking.

What fun it is to start clearing and planting again. I

find it is the breath of life for me to have a new project – dampened only by the thought that I shall probably not live long enough to see it all grow to maturity! But I am hopeful my children and grandchildren will.

Lavinia Cholmondeley

53   Part of Bakewell's wrought iron balustrade taken from the Old Hall in 1801. The sunken moat garden, planted in 1977 with silver plants, was especially designed to show it off.

54   *Cardiocrinum giganteum* among a big, old group of bamboo.

55   A thirty-four year old *Catalpa bignonioides*.

56   The west tower of the Castle seen rising above an *Acer palmatum* 'Atropurpureum', flanked by mature golden yews. The grass is dappled with fallen 'pocket handkerchiefs' from the *Davidia involucrata*, top right. Rose moyesii 'Superba' and 'Nevada' below.

Mrs Jill Cowley's garden, GREAT WALTHAM, ESSEX

Park Farm stands above the River Chelmer and one of the reasons I bought it was the view across the river into perfect parkland. The house, hundreds of years old, had been occupied by tenants for 300 years; the garden contained just a few ancient apple trees, a sixty-year-old walnut, a magnificent and hoary yew which towers over the house and some scruffy old box.

On the day I viewed the house, the land was running with rabbits. The grass was closely cropped to look like lawn, which should have been a warning to me. An old barn on the roadside, intended to serve as garages and a marvellous background for tender plants, collapsed the very day I signed the contract, closing the road for two days and leaving piles of rubble, tiles and old, immensely heavy timbers all over the ground in front of the house.

It was two years before I really began to garden, although in my spare moments I planted a yew hedge to enclose a rectangle of garden facing the living-room window. One of my first tasks was to plant the trees I wanted to get growing. In went two cedars, a taxodium, catalpa, yews, wellingtonias, three metasequoias, *Acer davidii* and *A. grosseri hersii*, a medlar, a quince, a mulberry and many more.

Architect Derek Bracey took over the planning and drew up a design, as well as moving all the enormously heavy barn timbers on rollers to form a terrace outside the living room. He and my son Andrew found a York

stone cattle trough behind another barn, which was still standing, and reconstructed it for the terrace. For paving we used old bricks which littered the whole site from the vast complex of barns that had stood there years before. The foundations of the fallen barn were impossible to remove, so these were left and the fallen bricks collected and used to build interior retaining walls, where I grow alpines backed by larger shrubs and lilies in a long border.

Now the garden is on three levels. We have divided it up into many separate 'rooms'. The terrace garden, with mostly white flowers and silver foliage, is one of my most successful plantings – in my eyes at least. In front of the yew hedge I put a cutting of *Salix exigua*, which now has to be cut back each year for its fine filigree silver foliage. The salix is underplanted with crambe, *Campanula alliariifolia* 'Ivory Bells', *Campanula burghaltii* and Iceberg roses with white geraniums, senecio and a *Viburnum plicatum* 'Lanarth'. The yew hedge is already six feet high, and the white poplar I planted on the bank behind it with a *Salix alba argentea* (syn. *S.a. sericea*) makes a marvellous combination of whites, silvers and forest greens.

In contrast there is the plain walk between the box hedge, passing through the yew hedge, down a flight of steps and up a slight bank to end at two tall poplars, grown from cuttings of trees from Fez in Morocco, an idea copied from the writings of Vita Sackville-West. At each intersection there are views up and down and across to the big rose garden, the tapestry hedge walk – rather a grand title, as the hedge plants are only twelve inches high at the moment – through into the Chinese garden and on into a paddock.

There is a winter garden by the kitchen door with

57 A small gravel and brick-paved garden where the flowering season starts with anemones, white muscari and species tulips. In June, roses 'Natalie Nypels', 'Céleste' and 'Raubritter', with pinks, lilies and *Nicotiana sylvestris* scent the air. A young *Cercidiphyllum japonicum*, a group of *Aralia elata*, a paulownia and a *Pinus bungeana* add interest.

Hamamelis 'Pallida', *Mahonia* 'Charity' and *M. japonica*, sarcococcas, *Viburnum* 'Park Farm', Bowles's golden grass, *Iris foetidissima*, hundreds of snowdrops and aconites and many hellebores.

My donkey Benjamin is also my compost heap. His manure has transformed what was a cobbled cattle yard at the front of the house, where the cow barn once stood. It was impossible to dig when we came. Rough grass grew over the hard core of centuries, packed down to keep the animals standing on dry ground. In desperation we laid the rougher timbers from the barn on the ground in the rough shapes of flower borders, laid newspapers over the grass, and then layered on the muck from Benjamin's barn. That was five years ago. Every year year I have mulched with Benjy's manure and there is now almost as much soil as there is stone. The great success has been the shrub roses, 'Maigold', 'Canary Bird' and 'Nevada', which have all become massive bushes and flower profusely even though they appear to be growing in a building site. Now the yard is called the 'hot' garden because, by accident, I seem to have planted red, orange, yellow and some white plants there.

Most of my garden came into being by accident, except for the now careful planning of the 'bones' by

Derek. There is a dairy building close by the house which was Gothicked many years ago by the land-owner to look picturesque from his own stately home. It had a small area of grass to itself, fronting a steep bank down to a large pond. It was windswept and difficult, but had the only good soil in the garden. Here I planted the paulownia, a sophora, an *Actinidia chinensis*, as well as *Rosa longicuspis* to grow up the verandah and shade the building from the hot sun.

The whole effect, with the steeply curved roof of the dairy, was rather Chinese. I was fortunate enough to make a trip to that marvellous country, and came back with a lot of (legal) cuttings. Now I have a Chinese garden of my own. It was designed to look rather like one I saw in Suchow, with paving, gravel, pots of asters and lilies, some bonsai on slate, a water tank and as many cuttings as survived, including two roses. I have ordered a *Pinus bungeana*, which has marvellous patchy bark and the quality of a Chinese drawing, to grow in one corner, and have planted eremurus, peonies, incarvillea, more lilies, roses: *R. willmottiae* and the threepenny bit rose, *Rosa elegantula* 'Persetosa' (syn. *R. farreri persetosa*).

I think I love the roses best. Every piece of the garden now has one or two, mostly old shrub roses. Rose

'Alba Semiplena' once dropped a seedling that, for some reason, I potted on. It is now a magnificent eight-foot by eight-foot, with slender stems crowded on a strong root. I have just planted *Rosa richardii* (*R. sancta*) because it is the oldest rose in history, and because of its Ethiopian roots. Other favourite roses are the Pemberton musks, which 'furnish' a garden with great swags of flower, just like comfortable English chintz. Massed old roses are underplanted with geraniums in all the soft shades, catmint, lavender, eremurus, phormium for architectural interest and as many silver plants as I can cram into the front of the borders. I do like the strong-growing modern roses like 'Chinatown', 'Queen Elizabeth', 'Golden Wings', 'Cerise Bouquet' and, particularly, 'Iceberg', to fill in the backs of borders in the later summer months when my darlings have finished.

I find rue, santolina and senecio indispensable for edging and making groups for continual shape and colour, and I find I am sympathetic to giant plants, probably because I am rather big myself. I grow petasites, peltiphyllum, rodgersias, rheums, *Heracleum mantegazzianum* and gunnera in a great wild mass at the bottom of the pond garden, where they can thug each other unmercifully. My favourite giant is *Crambe cordifolia* and I have placed a mass of them on a bank above the ponds for a spectacular effect in June. They are planted with various species of philadelphus, so the effect is three-storied: massive crambe leaves, huge crambe flower heads, with the philadelphus flowers nodding over the top.

I may say, 'That's it, I'm going to give up gardening' – after a particularly dreadful winter; or when I visit someone else's lovely garden and know I can never emulate it; when I have to work long hours and miss seeing the garden for a whole day – yet hope springs as I plan, cunningly, to garden the edges of Benjamin's paddock next year. I could fit in a few more roses there . . .

Jill Cowley

60

58 White 'Triumphator' tulips shine in the early May morning light by the dairy. *Dicentra spectabalis* and its white form, and the silvery leaves of artemisias and pinks are accented by the recently planted yew hedge which will frame a view to the village.

59 A quiet composition in greens and golds in a secret garden made on the floor of a demolished barn. An *Acer* 'Drummondii' shadows banks of *Euphorbia wulfenii* and *Verbascum olympicum* flowers on its tall spires. *Aesculus parviflora* blooms in the background in July and the young yellow Leylandii is one of a line to be clipped into cylinders.

60 The old farmhouse seen through the branches of an ancient apple tree which is festooned with Rose 'Seagull' in July and scarlet Virginia creeper in autumn. 'China Pink' tulips underplanted with *Geranium* 'Johnson's Blue' are planted in front of a *Malus floribunda*. In the background, another old apple is wreathed – in season – with roses 'Albertine', 'Complicata' and 'Mme Plantier'.

The Lady Margaret Fortescue's garden, BARNSTAPLE, DEVON

I hardly know how to begin to write about the garden as I did not make it. I have been lucky enough to inherit a garden created by my ancestors two hundred years ago and now at full maturity. No violent changes have taken place. True, trees have grown, follies have tumbled and the walled kitchen garden is a shadow of what it was. But essentially my garden today was made between 1750 and 1780 – and I love it the way it is.

It evolved like this. Tired of court politics Hugh, 1st Lord Fortescue, forsook London for his country estate in North Devon and decided to transform his manor house into a classical Palladian mansion and to make a formal garden in the manner of Le Nôtre. Lord Burlington advised him on the former but his own knowledge and inspiration decided the latter.

The house is sited on a shelf under a hill. On the top of the hill he built a ruined Gothick castle from which the house takes its name. In front of the house he devised a series of sloping grass terraces which descend into the valley where he made a large cruciform pond of about one and a half acres. On the other side of the pond a grand walk led up the opposite hill (and still does) to culminate in a Triumphal Arch on the horizon. This was a formal French concept, where the eye was directed to look straight ahead and not allowed to wander. Tight tree planting on each side ensured this.

Then ideas began to change. The English landscape garden made its debut. Like many others, Matthew, 2nd Lord Fortescue, was susceptible to the new fashion. So the serried ranks of trees were broken up, a series of garden buildings constructed to divert the eye, and the cruciform pond was reshaped to become part

of a serpentine river. His most fanciful idea was to flood some meadows and 'shred' the surrounding trees so that, from the house, it would look like a port complete with the masts of ships. At Castle Hill today you can see some of these follies, still barely altered. I have inherited a garden in the grand manner. Various writers have attributed the design to William Kent or Charles Bridgeman but exhaustive research has shown nothing of the sort. It seems to me certain that what was done was planned and effected by Hugh and Matthew Fortescue and their brilliant agent, Mr Hilliard. At all events, I feel it would be presumptuous of me to try to alter matters.

What I have done is preserve the design and add to the planting. The first thing was to restore and rebuild the Triumphal Arch; the latest has been to convert two rather ugly stone basins on the terrace, which were previously filled with annuals, into pools each with a lead fountain of a boy and a swan.

I have said that I try to preserve the design, but I do listen to all advice. It is too easy to sit in a deckchair or wander along a familiar path without noticing the stealthy advance of nature. As an example, I have a particularly charming temple which is the focal point as one comes up the drive. Around it had grown and progressively expanded a large belt of rhododendrons. I had become accustomed to walking around the belt to see the temple until a friend pointed out how the site was being overwhelmed, and that I must take drastic action to restore the *status quo*. A few years ago John Codrington cast his expert eye over the garden and he came up with all sorts of ideas, some of which are being gradually phased in. His plans are veritable masterpieces and I have had them beautifully bound

61 View from the cliff.

62

63

by a charming friend, Rosalind Campbell.

It has been great fun to develop and extend the planting in a fairly sheltered valley to the west of the house. This ends in an arboretum which, incidentally, contains what I am told is the largest Sitka spruce in the country. It is an extraordinary specimen with pendulous branches which have layered and become forty-foot trees in their own right. But it is on the area around the stream that I have concentrated, planting magnolias, camellias, halesias, eucryphias, pittosporums, pieris, rhododendrons, viburnums, astilbes, acers, wiegelas, mahonias, primulas et cetera. These flank a gravel path which runs alongside the stream to end in a rustic, jagged stone bridge unkindly called Ugly Bridge. Opposite it is a little Doric temple and, close by, a gloomy grotto called Sybil's Cave, which my mother filled in because she thought it was dangerous, but which I am determined to excavate and rebuild. I have also developed and opened up the cliff behind the house. In all this I was greatly helped by two dear friends, Anthony and Dorothy Sandford, now alas both dead, who lived here, loved the place and spent many hours working in the garden. We bought nearly all our plants from West Country gardens but not many from the Cornish ones as we felt they would not be hardy enough.

Please don't assume that all Devon is balmy or sub-tropical. Here it is often very cold, we have an annual rainfall of forty-five inches, and we are in a frost pocket and totally exposed to the prevailing south-west wind. Honey fungus is an appalling menace and we lose things every year to it. To my sorrow, it has just attacked and destroyed 'Julian Williams' 'Lawrence', 'John' and 'Philip' rhododendrons, named after three of his head gardeners and which he gave me as tiny plants twenty-five years ago. I also lost an enormous *Eucryphia* 'Nymansay', which really did look lovely during the summer. The place is infested with rabbits and moles which are no help; neither were the pheasants until I persuaded the shoot to rear their birds further away from the garden.

I have a marvellous gardener, Michael Toze, whose father was head gardener here for thirty-one years. He has an excellent part-time assistant, Charlie Rippon. Michael was born here, has worked here all his life and, even though he has never had any formal training, he is a natural, most successful at propagating and taking layers and an intrepid mover of quite large shrubs. When we find things are getting too big we start developing another area and move them into it –

64

instant gardening at its best and very successful nine times out of ten. Michael works all hours and is full of good ideas; it is seldom that I do not agree with his suggestions. We both read as many gardening magazines and books as we can. I like to think that my ancestors knew best and that what you can see here today is their brainchild and my lucky stewardship. My daughter and son-in-law are keen gardeners and are a great help to me in planning for the future. It is very comforting to know that the garden will continue to be developed and looked after by them.

Margaret Fortescue

62 The view looking up at the cliff from the front door, with old rhododendrons planted by earlier generations.

63 A carpet of bluebells beside the steps leading down to the stream.

64 The Ugly Bridge and, under a cascade of Rose 'Paul's Himalayan Musk', the Doric temple.

65 View looking south over the terraces to the triumphal arch at the end of the vista.

65

Mrs E. N. Pumphrey's garden, LISS, HAMPSHIRE

After many years in the Royal Navy travelling the world, my husband left the Service and we came to live in this delectable corner of Hampshire, at Greatham Mill; he was to satisfy a long-felt craving to farm and I was to make a garden. Both of us were almost totally ignorant, full of enthusiasm and, happily, considerably younger than we are now.

What I set out to do those thirty years ago (and am still doing) was to create a 'cottage' garden which, I felt, would be in keeping with the old, pink brick house. Quite apart from that, it is absolutely my favourite type of garden. I would probably have done the same if we had fetched up in a concrete box.

So, to the preliminaries. I joined the Royal Horticultural Society, took out a subscription to a weekly gardening magazine, bought some tools and thankfully threw away my Navy cocktail party clothes. I wish I could say that at this stage I had had the soil analysed and carefully noted . . . Not at all. I had never heard of pH and could not have told potash deficiency from scarlet fever. I discovered in time that the soil here is heavy clay and alluvial deposit, neutral and now much improved through the years with annual mulches of cow manure donated by a generous son-in-law from his healthy cows. Instead, I stood at our bedroom window and looked long and hard at what is now our 'front garden'. What I saw from this vantage point filled me with excitement. The potential was terrific: roughly triangular in shape, the apex away from the house, bounded on one side by the River Rother, on the other side by the tail-race from the mill,

66 Two beds border a straight grass path in the front garden. On the left, in the foreground, is *Amsonia salillicifolia*; on the right, a bank of *Rosa alba* 'Great Maiden's Blush'.

with a beautiful old wall along the front. Nothing much in the garden but Michaelmas daisies, golden rod and dozens of apple trees.

A clean sweep was the answer. Again, I wish I could say I laid my plans all drawn out on squared paper in an organised fashion . . . Oh no! Out I strode with blissful confidence, armed to the teeth with my shiny new tools.

Many and dire were the mistakes, and the poor plants had little peace, being continually yanked out and moved around. It took me ages to realise that my little collection of pygmies would grow. Anyway, after some years we had two island beds and a half-moon-shaped shrub border with raised alpine beds all along the old wall.

Everyone, I suppose, has favourite shrubs and so do I. But I am desperately unfaithful, I fear, and 'grow out' of certain plants. For example, *Elaeagnus pungens* 'Maculata', which was an original pygmy in the shrub border and described in Hilliers' manual as of 'moderate growth'. Moderate growth be blowed! It is enormous and shiny and gold; I flinch whenever I pass it. On the other hand, I am besotted with every single daphne and firmly believe this is 'till death . . .'

We start off with *Daphne pontica* of the greeny-yellow divinely scented tassels, then move on to *D. cneorum* and *D.c.* 'Variegata'. These last two are prostrate, smothered in pink and white flowers with an unearthly scent. And on to *D. genkwa*, an oriental shrub difficult to establish and a beast to propagate. But the leafless branches are swathed in lilac flowers in May. Then there is *D. x burkwoodii* 'Somerset', fast growing and deliciously fragrant. And then *D. collina* and *D. x neapolitana*, lovely rock garden shrubs.

67

68

You will conclude that I am fond of daphnes; but think deeply before planting any of these glorious shrubs. They loathe being moved. Resist also the almost irresistible temptation to cut too many of the gorgeous scented flowers, and chase away, with oaths and guns if necessary, predatory flower arrangers.

I also made a water garden in the tail-race. This meant getting rid of some charming ducks we had inherited, but I hoped the water garden would compensate in time. My favourite plants in this watery place are, I think, the ligularias, 'Othello' and 'Desdemona', great shaggy orange daisies flowering so agreeably late in the year; also their close relation, a lovely thing with golden feathery spires, black stems, striking and impressive – *L. przewalskii*.

So there was a dear, easily-looked-after little garden. Enough, you might say, but the bug had bitten deep. There was a field behind our house – virgin land full of tussocky grass, thistles, docks and the occasional cow. All we had to do was to open the gate . . .

We did just that. I say 'we' because Jim Collins joined the strength about then, a young, strong and intelligent gardener whose help and hard work through the years have been superb; also that of his heavenly wife Elsie. Above all, there was my husband, who is an admirable garden boy, totally encouraging and supportive, although he has been heard to murmur, 'Everyone, but everyone, is making their garden smaller except you.' Nevertheless, through that gate and into that field we plunged.

I should now explain that the water supply for the mill was by way of a leat, taken off from the river at a dam about a quarter of a mile above the garden. So in days gone by, in times of heavy rainfall, the millers turned the surplus water from the leat by means of a sluice-gate under a lovely old brick tunnel, and it flowed away under a humpy bridge to miss out the mill and rejoin the river. This, in millers' language, is a 'spillway'. And here we found the remains of those excellent and practical arrangements – buried, alas, under barrowloads of brambles, nettles, dandelions and the biggest docks in Hampshire. However, these obstacles were ultimately overcome and it is now a water-cum-wild garden, where primulas exult, as do hostas and great clumps of astilbe, grasses and rushes, and never-to-be-despised marsh marigolds, dug up originally from a ditch on the farm. This, I think, is definitely my favourite bit of the garden, even though it was horrendous to make and is tedious to maintain. It is hard work, fraught with acute discomfort and some peril. Do not for a second believe that a wild garden will look after itself. Far from it. Just turn your back and see what happens.

Now, twenty years or so on, we have quite a respectable garden of around one and a half acres. It is generally taken to be much bigger, because I designed it with many unexpected twists and turns, with seats at strategic points and a flight or two of steps leading the eye on, up or down. This back garden is jam-packed with shrubs, herbaceous plants, grasses, bulbs. More or less in the middle we have a small 'outcrop'. We can't grow proper alpines, because everything is too wet, but we have masses of 'rock plants': phloxes, aubretias and the like, and a few conifers at selected points.

I had the great experience for some years of working on the stand of Sherrards at the RHS shows in Vincent Square. Here, thanks to the patience and kindness of Brian Davies, I learnt the most tremendous amount about the glorious subject of trees and shrubs. Our most recent venture has been to create an 'arboretum' – I often garden above my station. This is away at the far end and we have some wonderful trees and shrub roses, with carpets of snowdrops, fritillaries, hardy cyclamen and polyanthus grown from the specialist seed supplied by Barnhaven in Cumbria. We also have a nursery, propagating and selling the plants which we grow in the garden. This has proved immensely popular, and I enjoy the days the garden is open, every Sunday afternoon from April until the end of September, but of course we also welcome visitors any day or time of the year if they make an appointment.

There is masses more virgin field, but my husband has caused a huge and high fence to be erected – not so much to keep the deer out as to keep me in.

67 A collection of standard and bush fuchsias which stand outside in a group in the summer.

68 The gateway made some thirty years ago to the back garden.

69 The Dell, which is permanently damp, where primulas, irises and mimulus flourish. Depending on the rainfall, there is a little stream running through the middle.

70 View towards the arboretum in the distance, with snowdrops, followed by fritilleries.

69

70

Mrs Reginald Sheffield's garden,
SUTTON-ON-THE-FOREST, YORKSHIRE

In 1961, when my husband and I realised that, sadly, it would be impossible for us to go on living in the vast Sheffield family house, Normanby in Lincolnshire, we decided that we would like to move only to somewhere else in the north of England. We both made three stipulations. Mine were that the house should be near a village, face south and have no long drives, since staff – if one were lucky enough to have them – should not be scared to walk home at night. My husband's were that it must have a farm in hand, have woodlands, and be in striking distance of Normanby, since, although he had let the house and park to the borough of Scunthorpe, he had kept the estate. We were lucky enough to be able to buy Sutton Park in Yorkshire in 1962 and to have all our desires fulfilled. We wanted to live in the north because it has all the shooting and racing that one could ever need, because we have so many friends here, and because I think Yorkshire the most beautiful county in England.

From my earliest childhood I have loved gardening, and when my husband bought Sutton, we immediately saw how we would plan the garden because of the two terraces that were already there. It is a Georgian house, built in the early eighteenth century, overlooking parkland designed by 'Capability' Brown. The centre block of the house has three stories, with two wings and a pavilion at each end. It faces south, with large shelter belts enclosing the park on both sides.

We moved into Sutton in August 1963. The year before was spent in pulling out many laurels and other evergreen shrubs which had been badly neglected, taking in a large piece of the park which included a beautiful cedar tree, planting a beech hedge to divide the garden from the park. We also got rid of all the gravel paths. There was no way into the garden on the south front except by a passage near the kitchen, and a hedge had been planted the whole way along the front of the house. This we pulled out and Francis Johnson, our architect, designed some very simple steps to come down from the centre library window. We got tons of flagstones from the kitchens of old houses in Otley and, with them, made a large terrace.

The only flowers I can remember in the garden were 'Alain' roses that had mostly gone back in briars. These made a narrow border running the whole length of the top terrace; we scrapped them and widened the border, planting it with some of my favourite things, keeping the colours to greys, pinks and mauves – *Anaphalis margaritacea*, *Artemisia arborescens*, santolina, senecio, acanthus, roses 'Magenta' and 'Prelude', pink and white mallow, heliotrope, Madonna lilies, pink and purple penstemons and six standard wisteria. At both ends of the terrace squares project towards the second terrace, on which we put white wire temples to give height and architectural interest. Up these I have grown 'Chaplin's Pink Climber' and *Clematis montana*, and in the beds around the temples I have planted the musk roses I love – 'Penelope', 'Prosperity' and 'Felicia', 'Lavender Lassie' (Kordes '60) and, my favourite, 'Constance Spry'. Under the windows on each side of the terrace, two more borders have been made and planted with highly-scented plants: nicotiana, standard heliotrope, honey-

71 Looking from beyond the water to the south front. *Chamaecyparis* 'Allumii', planted to give height, give an architectural air to the garden.

72

73

74

75

suckle and regale lilies and *Abutilon vitifolium*. All these are underplanted with *Mentha rotundifolia* and some with night-scented stocks, so that on a warm evening the whole house is filled with their wonderful scent. Up the walls of the house we grew *Jasminum officinale*, *Clematis flammula* ('Virgin's Bower') and wisteria.

On the second terrace an old friend, the garden designer Percy Cane, who created the wonderful garden at Dartington, laid out the beds. The centre-piece is a large stone fonthead moved from our old home, Normanby, which we fill with sweet-scented geraniums. The beds are planted with perennials and annuals: peonies, pinks, dicentra, stocks and low-growing shrub roses. In eight corner beds is a *Pyrus salicifolia* 'Pendula', which we prune to look like pale green umbrellas. On one side of the steps leading to this terrace, we planted white *Wisteria venusta*, which has such a delicious scent, and on the other a *Vitis vinifera* 'Brandt'. To the right and the left, at the bottom of these steps, the wide herbaceous borders are planted only in blue, yellow, white and grey. Towering over the terrace are two black iron statues of children.

One of the less desirable things I inherited was a rockery. I really hate alpines, so I planted it all over with green ground cover and it looks very well. The one thing that was missing in the garden was water so, on the new lawn below the second terrace, we made a long lily canal. We have kept this part of the garden quite formal, with no colour, only white petunias, *Helichrysum petiolatum*, *Ballota pseudodictamnus* and *Teucrium fruticans* in urns round the canal. Against the wall of the third terrace we planted *Chamaecyparis lawsoniana* 'Allumii', they have to be clipped every five years from scaffolding to ensure they keep their perfect columnar habit.

To the far left of this terrace, a small arboretum was

72 The lily canal was made when the garden was extended into the park. The fine cedar of Lebanon gave this new garden an instantly mature look.

73 The second terrace is planted either side of the steps with a wide herbaceous border. The smaller beds are kept in one colour, with the colours of all the beds blending.

74 A tree paeony with a *Viburnum plicatum* overlooking the *Artemisia arborescens*.

75 The early font head, with the twelve apostles round it. Weeping silver pear (*Pyrus salicifolia* 'Pendula') have been trained and cut like green umbrellas. The shrub roses have grown through them.

created with liquidambars and metasequoias, which are doubly attractive as they will have superb autumn colouring. Equally lovely is the snake-barked acer and *Aesculus indica* (the Indian horse chestnut) and, surprisingly, a very sturdy looking *Eucryphia* x *nymansensis*. I had always thought it too tender a tree for our northern temperatures, but it has flourished and flowered very well after eight years. Beyond this grove is a pergola, which I have planted with laburnum only. I have always longed to have a tunnel of this; I think it is a lovely tree which is much despised by most gardeners. This leads to another woodland walk strewn with Lent lilies, bluebells and primroses and carpeted with snowdrops and aconites.

To the west, we made a border of irises, phlox, Rugosa roses and buddlejas to attract butterflies. To the east, you approach a semi-wild glade which goes for nearly half a mile to a temple; it is planted with nothing but white flowering shrubs. The whole length on either side is filled with narcissus and daffodils. I was fortunate enough to find a background of lovely white cherries. On the approach to this walk, many woodland plants flourish: giant-leaved *Gunnera manicata*, *Rheum palmatum* 'Atrosanguineum', the giant hemlock, *Heracleum mantegazzianum* (which I hope will seed and grow to ten feet), Solomon's Seal, hostas and *Bergenia cordifolia*. I am lucky that the soil, although light, seems to grow everything.

I let the 'Excelsior' strains of digitalis flower everywhere. I also have to have a large cutting garden to provide flowers for the house. Since we are open to the public from Easter till October, the main effort – really not so difficult – is to have colour for this period, starting with daffodils and ending with some of the new Michaelmas daisies. After three years of trial and tribulation I have learned to grow orchids quite successfully in a cool greenhouse and have made a good collection. Most of the greenhouse work I do myself, as I only have two gardeners and the mowing and edging seem to take up so much time.

Above all, I want the whole air of my garden scented with flowers with only the sound of the cooing of my white fantail pigeons, and the swallows and house martins dipping themselves in the lily canal. I can never feel lonely, as so many of my friends have given me plants and I feel as if they are almost there in the garden with me.

Nancie Sheffield

Mrs Basil Barlow's garden, DURSLEY, GLOUCESTERSHIRE

We first saw Stancombe twenty years ago on a late October morning – or, rather, at first we did not see it, as the whole area was shrouded in thick fog. After inspecting the house, there, suddenly, was the sun and the beautiful autumn colours of the woods against a deep blue sky. Sheep and cows were grazing in the valley, and the fields were like amphitheatres. This breathtaking view unfolded before our eyes; then and there we decided that this was where we wanted to live. We had not even seen the garden or the farm.

The garden seemed vast. There was a garden around the house, then further down the valley a folly garden, a lake (or rather three!), and a much neglected kitchen garden – about fifteen acres in all. However were we going to manage all this, especially as we had been told that there had been seven gardeners only a decade before? We did not know then that we were to inherit a splendid man, Kenneth Brown, who had worked at Stancombe all his life. Now, all these years later, he, my husband and I, and of course up-to-date machinery, make a good team to keep the place in order.

I have always been keen on growing things, and as children we were much encouraged to know the names of flowers in the fields. One knew garden flowers, of course, although varieties were limited. At Stancombe in the beginning I had professional help to avoid costly and time-consuming mistakes and, also, where changes were needed, to achieve the necessary good bone structure. The vision and expertise of Lanning Roper, Peter Coats and Fred Whitsey were invaluable for the realisation of the garden today.

76 *Allium karataviense, Geranium* 'Johnson's Blue', *Euonymus fortunei* 'Silver Queen' and a *Rosa rugosa* 'Frau Dagmar Hartopp' surround a marble statue.

Having established that, we were able to indulge in planting schemes. When planting, one aims to create compositions with form, colour and texture. It is not unlike a painting. If you have a view, which must be considered for an overall pleasing effect, it should not be spoilt by an elaborate and colourful planting, for this draws the eye away from the whole picture. The planting must mould into the countryside and echo the lovely folds of the land. It should be a harmonious part of the surroundings. The use of subtle colours – grey, lime green – and of variegated plants and shrubs with flowers of white, pink, mauve, purple and pale lemon enhances the whole conception.

We only retained two large herbaceous borders from the former lay-out. They lie across an indentation of the field which runs almost to the house. In order to accentuate the view from the front door, steps have been put in, up a small bank, flanked by three *Taxus baccata, Senecio* 'Sunshine', *Cotinus coggygria, Cornus alba* 'Elegantissima' and *C.a.* 'Spaethii', and other shrubs, to give a tapestry effect. This is continued on the right side of the house, again slightly elevated, where in recent years we have removed a large Turkey oak which, after the drought of 1976, was leaning dangerously towards the house, and replaced it with a gazebo, over which a rose and *Actinidia kolomikta* are slowly climbing.

There are well-established large cedars and sweet chestnuts encircling the whole area and, at the far end, a row of *Thuja plicata* acts as a windbreak, much needed as we have lost several huge trees in near-hurricane gales, while the Dutch elm disease has left devastating gaps. A large marble urn is set in the middle of the upper lawn, surrounded by a low box

hedge, with golden privet for winter colour and lilies and hostas inside. This in turn is encircled by twelve *Acer pseudoplatanus* 'Worleei', with an opening leading to another vista via a row of pleached limes. Here a Chinese bench is flanked by four cherubs, with *Osmanthus delavayi*, *O. heterophyllus* and *Hebe rakaiensis* billowing out around them. This used to be a rose garden, and indeed there are still a lot of roses, but today they tend to be old-fashioned shrub roses and roses rambling over trees. 'Francis E Lester', 'Seagull', 'Rambling Rector' are favourites, and a few Hybrid Musk roses – 'Penelope' and 'Prosperity' – make a curved hedge within a criss-cross white fence.

More shrub roses border the path towards the folly garden. Historically, this is the most interesting part of the estate. A walk descending down steps to a single row of York flagstones winds, eventually, around the largest of the three lakes, complete with tunnels and grottoes. On the way, a font and Grecian temple add to the mysterious setting. Sometimes I find pieces of mosaic surfacing, as a Roman villa once stood here, and the buildings bear testimony to earlier finds. The folly garden was built at the time of the Napoleonic wars, at the beginning of the nineteenth century. The owner, so the story goes, had a rich and portly wife,

who could not manage the steep descent and narrow paths, and was therefore unable to interrupt his tryst in the secret garden with a local gypsy girl. An idyllic setting for such a liaison, but whether true it matters not. Evelyn Waugh, who lived a mile away, wrote a large part of *Brideshead Revisited* sitting by the lake.

Why it was so fashionable to plant the common laurel, *Prunus laurocerasus*, in such profusion I can never understand. We are replacing them with more interesting shrubs, retaining only a few to form low coverings for banks. There are wonderful copper beeches, yews, various varieties of salix, a liquidambar and *Metasequoia glyptostroboides*, and a small acer collection on the south-west side of the lake – *Acer capillipes*, *ginnala*, 'Sango Kaku', *circinatum* and others.

Elsewhere we have a cornus collection, in its early stages, the ones with bright coloured stems which thrive on alkaline soil; huge *Gunnera manicata* and many of the useful bogplants for ground cover (*Petasites japonicus giganteus* is a bit too rampant for my liking and has to be curbed); many lacecap hydrangeas, and much more.

Drifts of bulbs would look lovely in the woodlands, but unfortunately the heavy clay soil is stony and

difficult to work in places. Luckily we have a good supply of horse and cow manure from the farm, and I am forever buying large bales of peat. We take a lot of trouble to make big planting holes for precious new shrubs and trees. *Ptelea trifoliata* 'Aurea', *Chionanthus virginicus*, and a golden and a purple Dawyck beech have just gone in.

How easy it is to erase an unwanted effect on the canvas with a stroke of the spatula, but quite another matter to undo the things which do not please you in the garden. I fear that I am forever moving things. When yet another move is mentioned, Kenneth may well throw his eyes to the sky and I do not blame him, but he never shows any impatience, for which I am grateful. We have even moved twelve-year-old trees with the greatest success.

I enjoy a good dig – physical exertion makes the satisfaction of a job well done all the more intense. At the same time the mind is active too. This is the moment when I 'write' my letters to *The Times*. It has become a habit when walking the dogs to view everything with a critical eye, wondering and pondering how to improve – whether to lighten up an area (I like the use of masses of white or apricot foxgloves and have got them everywhere) or to discard an old outgrown shrub. I like to imagine new vistas or think of new projects. These are the real pleasures of gardening. There are sometimes sudden inspirations, exciting feelings, when one would like to go to work immediately. It might be to try to grow a *Rosa webbiana* next to an existing *Juniperus virginiana* 'Grey Owl' with a clematis rambling through it. Time will tell whether it is a success or not. Inspiration also comes from chance remarks of friends, reading and learning from the excellent selection of garden books now available, and of course from visiting other gardens.

Talking of pleasures, there are the delicious moments when wafts of scent stop you in your tracks to sniff the air. There is an abundance in June when species of philadelphus are in flower. These perhaps are my favourites, though the honeysuckles, especially *Lonicera japonica* and *L. periclymenum*, rambling

77 A view from the house towards the herbaceous borders, with a white painted seat flanked by *Catalpa bignonioides* 'Aurea', and *Populus candicans* 'Aurora'.

78 An eighteenth-century urn surrounded by clipped golden privet with lilies and a *Clematis* 'Duchess of Edinburgh' climbing up the base of the urn. The whole is encircled by *Acer pseudoplatanus* 'Worleei'.

79

80

81

82

over tree stumps, have an outstanding fragrance. Each season has its 'specials'; even winter ones are powerful and most welcome on dreary grey days. *Chimonanthus praecox* can give you a special boost, as can viburnum and osmanthus. I adore the curious smell of *Populus balsamifera*. There are the obvious: roses, lilies, sweet peas, the spicy perfumes of carnations and stocks, when you bury your nose in them and get deliciously drunk. Oh, and I must not forget my early spring delight in the greenhouse, *Jasminum officinale. Rhododendron* 'Fragrantissimum' . . . The list is endless. All that, and all the various activities, however backbreaking at times, make gardening a wonderful hobby. It has given me countless hours of happiness, and I hope that the many visitors from home and abroad who come here share these pleasures too.

I am keen on nature conservation: to observe, love and cherish plant and wild life is a privilege and essential in this materialistic age. Out of sight are acres of nettles and brambles, where the wild life can take over, live and breed undisturbed.

As I write it is October again. No trace of fog or mist outside this time. It is one of those rare days of intense colouring – sharp contrasts of almost black, grey and white bulbous clouds, shafts of sunshine coming out of

79 The Greek temple (*c.* 1820) and lake are part of a folly garden, an outstanding feature of the gardens at Stancombe. *Salix alba Argentea* and *Gunnera manicata* can be seen.

80 A view towards the lake with two large specimens of *Fagus sylvatica* – the common beech – and F. s. *purpurea*. In spring the slopes are covered with blue bells and wild garlic.

81 A newly planted bed, adjoining the borders, with *Digitalis purpurea alba* and *Yucca filamentosa*. The cedar of Lebanon was badly damaged by heavy snow and gales.

82 Part of the bog garden with *Iris sibirica, Rheum palmatum* 'Atropurpureum', petasites, *Peltiphyllum peltatum* and *Vibernum plicatum* 'Mariesii' in the background.

deep blue pockets in the sky, illuminating parts of the countryside below. There are incredible hues of gold. Suddenly, out of nowhere, a huge flock of seagulls descends on the fields, like a snowstorm against the black clouds. It is now, when I look incredulously onto this scene, that I rise out of myself, observe the view from a higher level – euphoria. Is this a glimpse into Paradise?

Gerda Barlow

Mrs James Lees-Milne, BADMINTON, AVON

Until my husband took me to Sissinghurst in 1952, where I met for the first time Vita Sackville-West, I had really no idea what gardening was all about. At the time we were living in France, but every visit to England took me back to Sissinghurst. I learnt to 'look' at plants, to understand about grouping them and how important colour schemes are. Vita was wonderfully patient with my idiotic questions and I got to know that extraordinary garden really well. From then on I read endless books, articles and horticultural catalogues, visited as many other gardens as possible and tried to improve my own stony, sun-baked patch above the Mediterranean.

A few years later we bought a house in Gloucestershire, where I started to create a very different type of garden. In those days plants were infinitely cheaper than they are today and friends were wonderfully generous. There was a lot of ground to cover, but after five years of hard work it began to take shape. The first thing I did was to put in trees and hedges as the background and bones of what was to come.

In our present garden at Badminton such planting was not necessary – nor even possible, as conditions are very different. After some ten years, including three very severe winters and a major drought, we once again have to count the cost of another arctic winter and spring. As I write, many things above ground, with the exception of roses – and some of them look in pretty bad shape – seem to be past hope of recovery and endless replacements will have to be found.

The garden, which is roughly half an acre, 600 feet

up with no protection from gales, is dominated by three ancient cedars of Lebanon. Of course they are lovely, but they do create problems. Needles rain down everywhere, with the result that the lawn never looks really green. Then there are the broken cones, which need constant sweeping up. After years of hard work I have got grass to grow under them and have planted masses of cyclamen, *C. hederifolium*, *cilicium* and *C. coum*; *Narcissus* 'Mount Hood' and *N.* 'Beersheba', because I prefer the white to the yellow; various Poeticus narcissi, scillas and, almost best of all, *Anemone blanda* 'Atrocaerulea', which have obligingly spread. When the sun reaches them and they turn up their faces the effect is ravishing. Crocuses seed themselves, but not enough, and snowdrops frankly don't care for the place.

Where there are gaps between the cedars and the sun and rain can penetrate, I have planted, at random, shrub roses such as 'Fritz Nobis', Gallica 'Complicata' and 'Charles de Mills', and *R. moyesii* 'Geranium', *R. californica* 'Plena' and the rambler 'Veilchenblau'. Another rambler, 'Bobbie James', now has a large frame for support and is a cascade of white flowers in late summer. Here too there are a few shrubs: *Viburnum plicatum mariesii* and *V. opulus* 'Xanthocarpum', which in autumn is loaded with translucent golden berries looking like luscious grapes. Two small *Prunus subhirtella* 'Autumnalis' and a *Gleditsia triacanthos* 'Sunburst' also share this difficult terrain. The latter is an excellent tree for a small garden and always lives up to its name.

Fortunately when we moved here I brought quite a lot of clipped box pyramids and balls. Today they are an astronomical price and quite difficult to find. Hav-

83 Apollo, lyre in hand, contemplates the house and village.

84

85

86

87

ing removed them from their tubs, I have placed them at strategic points in the garden. They also help punctuate the design of a formal arrangement in the centre of the lawn. The flagstones were already there, forming a sort of semi-circle on each side of the axial path. I edged the whole thing with box and placed the pyramids symmetrically. A smaller form of box edging follows the pattern inside and the space between them is filled with *Stachys olympica*, thymes, creeping campanulas, helianthemums and various other low-growing plants and bulbs, including species tulips, chionodoxas and scillas. At the four corners of this curious arrangement I have standard hollies, *Ilex x altaclaerensis* 'Golden King'. The hollies and the box are a joy in winter when everything else disappears or looks sad and tatty. I also think that in a small garden a certain amount of formality is necessary, so this idea is continued along the axial path which divides the lawn. On each side are six pairs of pyramids of variegated box. These took a long time to bush out, for variegated plants seem to grow more slowly.

In the four corners of the lawn are, at one end, two *Amelanchier laevis* and, at the other, two *Pyrus salicifolia* 'Pendula', planted in 1977 for the Queen's Silver Jubilee. The amelanchiers are good for small gardens, as they do not get out of hand, nor do they create too much shade. They are also lovely when wreathed in white flowers in early May, and in autumn when their leaves turn scarlet. Though perhaps less spectacular than the prunus family when in flower, they are much more attractive during the rest of the year.

There is one long raised border facing west. It was there when we came, but I have made a path of brick and stone down the middle – I find very wide beds too difficult to manage. It is backed by a four-foot boundary wall, on top of which I put trellis. Here there is an assortment of shrubs, herbaceous plants and climbers – *Abutilon x suntense*, *Cytisus battandieri*,

84 Various hostas flop over the stone and brick path which divides the raised border.

85 From the house, a bird's eye view across the lawn towards the dark cedars.

86 A clipped box pyramid stands on either side of the steps to the big border. Rose 'Constance Spry' can be seen sprawling along the wall.

87 In the so-called dry bed near the house, *Euphorbia cyparissias* spreads all too easily and the golden hop (*Humulus lupulus aureus*) rapidly smothers part of the house in summer.

piptanthus, ceanothus (constantly being killed by severe frosts), various shrub roses and many clematis, both large and small. On the side adjoining the path are more roses, interspersed with perennials and more herbaceous things: campanulas, white *Dicentra spectabilis*, white polemonium, several forms of cistus, lots of grey plants and different varieties of hosta. Alliums – *AA. christophii* (*A. albopilosum*), *giganteum* and *rosenbachianum* – have spread considerably, and in the very front there are small rock plants and trailing things. A rose I find most useful is a Centifolia 'Rose de Resht', a Persian shrub brought back years ago from Resht by Nancy Lindsay. The flowers are not very big but are a rich crimson and very recurrent. This rose is totally trouble-free, so I have several.

In a long, north-facing bed bordering the lawn but overshadowed by the cedars I wanted light things, so put in several white flowering shrubs – *Philadelphus coronarius* 'Aureus', *Hydrangea paniculata* 'Grandiflora' and *H.p.* 'Praecox', underplanted with variegated hostas, *Viola cornuta alba* and so forth. There are two wooden tripods for roses – 'Climbing Iceberg' and 'Golden Showers'. Here of course the dryness is a problem and constant watering is needed in summer.

A matching long bed at the opposite end of the lawn facing south has a mixture of shrub roses: 'Petite de Hollande', which is so pretty when in bud, 'Céleste', 'Koenigin von Dänemarck', 'Ispahan', 'William Lobb', 'Honorine de Brabant' and others, with one or two of 'The Fairy', useful in late summer. Some lilies and some of the taller alliums will obligingly grow through the roses, using them for support.

Copying that great gardener John Treasure, I have lately added a few clematis to thread their way in and out at random. The roses do not seem to suffer.

There is a small paved area by the house with a raised bed beside it. This is full of bulbs and special treasures, I have put down a lot of fine gravel, which seems to suit most of the occupants. Here too is a large *Rosa glauca* (*R. rubrifolia*), which is host to *Clematis* 'Royal Velours' – a splendid display in June.

I am very fond of all the honeysuckle family and grow several as standards. If you are short of space this can be a useful and pretty solution for many other plants as well. Along the west side of the lawn facing east is an ancient patchwork hedge of box and yew separating the garden from the road. Beneath it I have planted *Ruta graveolens* 'Jackman's Blue', which gives

a margin of colour to this sombre background. It needs hard clipping in April. Being acquisitive, I tend to buy plants on spec, so to speak, without any thought of where they will go. At times this garden is really full and at others, especially after a hard winter, very bare. I am also constantly moving plants.

Two *Hydrangea petiolaris* are doing well on the north side of the house, while the west side is smothered with an old wisteria and a rampant honeysuckle, with two wonderful clematis, 'Frances Rivis' and 'Perle d'Azur', filling every available space. On the south side where the wisteria also creeps round is that glorious early rose 'Madame Grégoire Staechelin', also climbers 'Madame Caroline Testout' and 'Gloire de Dijon'. In spring *Clematis* 'Miss Bateman' helps to cover one corner with its lovely pure white flowers and red centres. Further along, covering a somewhat unsightly addition to the house, the golden hop *Humulus lupulus aureus* and *Vitis coignetiae* grapple with each other, while beyond *Clematis cirrhosa balearica* (supposedly evergreen, but not here) camouflages the rest of the wall with its fern-like leaves and in winter, if we are lucky, tiny cream-coloured scented flowers.

To return to the end of the garden where the cedars are, two steps down take one into a small enclosed area. Here is a little oblong pond for fish and newts surrounded by pyramids and balls of box. Round the perimeter at one end are large bushes of *Philadelphus* 'Belle Etoile', *Viburnum carlesii*, *Hydrangea aspera villosa* and *H. paniculata grandiflora*. Primulas seem to flourish here, as the soil is moister and heavier than in the rest of the garden, and I am trying to grow as many varieties as possible. The wall behind is covered with various forms of variegated ivy. At the edge of the small lawn are four standard 'Iceberg' roses, while the west-facing side is filled with other shrubs and underplanted with *Lamium* 'Beacon Silver', campanulas and so forth.

The south-facing side is divided into narrow strips of pale yellow and white roses. The beds are separated by hexagonal stones. Along the back are six standard roses 'Pink Pearl', so pale they are almost white, very pretty and very prolific. The unattractive wooden fence which encloses three sides of this area is mostly hidden in summer by clematis, more variegated ivies, *Actinidia kolomikta*, one of my favourite roses, 'Alchemist', and other climbers.

I have to manage without manure, as there is nowhere to store it, and to my eternal shame I have never

89

90

been any good at compost heaps, so I only use Growmore, bonemeal, dried blood and Phostrogen. In summer I try to cover everything with a mulch of forest bark and peat to suppress weeds and hold moisture. There is no greenhouse.

My help is minimal and erratic and amounts to roughly twelve hours a week from Jane and Paul, who come when they can and are splendid. This does mean that most projects and alterations remain in my mind. Perhaps this is just as well.

88 Looking across the lawn and the formal parterre, which is surrounded by box edging and pyramids. Standard 'Golden King' hollies are at the four corners. Beyond is the big border with Badminton Park in the distance.

89 The small rectangular pond has clipped pyramids and walls of box around the margin.

90 At one end of the path dividing the raised border is a large specimen of rose 'Fantin Latour'. On the other side are *Allium albopilosum*, peonies and other herbaceous plants.

Alvilde Lees-Milne

85

Mrs Sean Cooper's garden, SHERSTON, WILTSHIRE

When I first saw this little derelict house, I more or less dismissed it as being too daunting a task to take on at my age. It had been a transport yard, with sheds and concrete all round the house, and about half an acre of tangled elder, old trees, nettles, stumps and brambles.

The house stands halfway up a hill on the outskirts of the village of Sherston, facing east and west, and to my delight, when I had struggled through the jungle, I found that there was a marvellous view to the west over a valley with a little stream at the bottom, across to the old village and far beyond.

My husband Sean was very optimistic, so we bought it and started at once to rebuild and add to the house. We found a marvellous, energetic farming friend, Mr Godwin, who came with his son and a tractor. They hauled out all the old concrete sheds, trees and endless rubbish, and we ourselves picked up and removed millions of stones. We kept just four very old trees, to give us a start: a yew, two apples and a cherry.

The next thing was to spray on a good dose of Tumbleweed, which seems to work best when the weeds are growing. Then, after ploughing, harrowing and levelling, we put on some more. This was a terribly important thing to do, as starting with clean ground makes an enormous difference to one's gardening life. I do the weeding myself and have never had any bad weeds in this new garden – no elder, docks or couch grass, and very little bindweed.

We moved into the house at Christmas 1980. There we were, faced with a large empty space sloping away

from the house in a peculiar wedge shape, with rather tumbledown walls, one of which, to my horror, ran straight across the garden between the house and the view. Luckily we had all the summer to think out the garden before planting in the autumn and, as I had had a bad hunting fall, there was plenty of time to sit and stare out of the window and make plans.

Sean had the brilliant idea of going for help to the labour exchange, where he found a splendid boy student. He looked strong, so I set him to work with a pickaxe quarrying out a lot of holes along this awful wall and filling them in with good soil, which had to be fetched from a field about three miles away. I was determined to plant at once some strong climbers – honeysuckle, *Hydrangea petiolaris*, roses, a vine, even cotoneasters – to cover the wall so that it would merge into the landscape.

In April we sowed the whole area with good grass seed, and, once it was established, we got some long ropes and laid them out on the ground in three huge, roughly kidney-shaped, beds. We left a grass path winding through the biggest bed to the bottom of the garden. The ground inside the ropes was then rota-vated and manured. The moment had arrived for me to think out the planting plan.

In spite of our lay-out, the garden still looked rather lopsided, so I decided to make a small formal area near the house: a square Cotswold stone terrace in front of our windows, with a low wall surrounding it, small plants in front – rock roses, alpine phlox, variegated ivies, aubrieta and so on – and a low hedge of Hidcote lavender behind the wall. A single step in the centre leads up to a square lawn surrounded by a yew hedge. Four golden yew balls mark the corners and a flat

91 *Clematis* 'Lasurstern' on the low terrace with Lavender 'Hidcote' behind and an urn filled with Geranium 'Duchess of Eastbourne'.

92

93

diamond-shaped stone the centre, with an urn full of bright flowers all summer. This year we have added three iron arches at the three exits from the yew hedge, and trained the rose 'Norwich Pink' and a clematis over each one – a gaudy splash of colour against the dark green of the yew. This square garden seems almost like an extension of the house, an outdoor room.

Sean is a terrific handyman and carpenter; he has made us a lovely little six-sided conservatory with a pointed roof and windows on all sides. We sit in it a great deal, surrounded by the garden. Inside it is always warm and sunny and out of the wind. He has also made a beautiful seat for the formal garden, and a most useful small yard, enclosed by trellis, for logs, coal and wheelbarrows, and this is now hidden by climbers.

We started planting the garden in October 1981, and filled the beds with shrubs, quite ordinary things: weigelas, philadelphus, strong-growing roses like musks, Rugosas, moss roses – even the rampant Rose '*Paulii*', to cover a manhole – and peonies, lilies, potentillas, geraniums, a lot of ground cover: really everything I liked and everything I was given by my friends. The boundary walls are covered with roses, vines, honeysuckle and clematis, which luckily have grown very well, and in summer it is a mass of colour.

I had to plant some rather dull, quick-growing cypresses in groups at the bottom of the garden, partly as a windbreak, partly to create a background for other plants. *Viburnum plicatum* 'Mariesii', taller roses, and such things as crambe and the golden cut-leaved elder look wonderful against the trees, but they have grown so fast that we have already had to cut their tops off and prune them severely. I now wish I had planted more interesting evergreens and not been so impatient. A point to remember.

I realise that I have planted far too many different things in my garden, and that a simple arrangement is usually the most effective, but in a small garden, seen continually from the house, there has to be a constant succession of flowers and foliage or there will be long dull phases. To get the best effect, tidiness is of the utmost importance – lawns mown, edges clipped and, in particular, dead wood and dead heads constantly removed. Luckily I love these routine jobs, and whilst doing them I can review and correct my mistakes.

I like to have various 'sitting' places in the garden. First there is the little terrace with a round white table and chairs, then the summer house, by far the most used. When it is really hot, we take chairs down under the old apple tree. Now I want even a fourth place, at the end of the garden, looking over the view and completely private.

We do all the work ourselves, except for a wonderful man, Mr Wally Watts, who has worked for me for many years. He is now retired, but comes one morning a week when it is fine. One drop of rain, and no Mr Watts. He is endlessly good-natured, and in three hours smartens up the garden in a most professional way. As the roses on the house have grown so tall, we have also had Mr Weaver to prune and arrange them for two mornings this year, as neither of us is much use on a high ladder.

For me, quite the worst job in the garden is staking and tying the roses and clematis. It is worth spending time and thought on the ways of doing this tidily and as permanently as possible. For very strong-growing roses, we have used four angle irons with cross pieces, and for others, and especially for the clematis, we make tripods. I suppose my chief mistake is the common one of planting the big shrubs much too close together. It is a bad mistake, as it becomes almost impossible to prune them hard enough without ruining their shape.

I visit a lot of gardens and nearly always get some ideas, very often in the most unlikely places. London gardens are marvellous, especially in the use of annuals and climbing plants. This garden at Sherston is the fifth I have created, and each time I am surprised and delighted to discover how quickly a hopeless site can become a pretty and maturing garden.

92 View from a bedroom window of yew hedges focusing on the old apple tree and white seat in the distance.

93 Rose 'Mme Grégoire Staechelin' climbs over the front door and new east wall of the house.

94 Black and White poppies with a dark-leaved *Weigela florida* 'Foliis Purpureis' in the foreground. Across the lawn, a yellow cut-leaved elder stands out, with Rose 'Marguerite Hilling' and a low yellow *Filipendula Ulmaria* 'Aurea'.

95 Red peonies with the yellow hop, *Humulus lupulus aureus*, on the fence behind.

94

95

Priscilla, Lady Bacon's garden, RAVENINGHAM, NORFOLK

My husband and a great friend and neighbour shared a pack of beagles which were kennelled at Raveningham. They both married about the same time and found that keeping wives as well as beagles was just not on. The wives won and the kennelman became our gardener. After one season he suggested to me that we have more of 'those plants of a beautiful blue that come up again next year'. I agreed that it was an excellent idea and bought some more delphiniums. We progressed from there. I read avidly and, if a great many books agreed that a certain plant, shrub or tree was first-class, I bought it. Of course this was sometimes disastrous, as I'd omitted to read about soil structure, climate and the pH values of soil. But I did at least know that we couldn't grow rhododendrons and azaleas.

As you approach the drive to Raveningham, the road takes a sharp bend to the right. The Bacon who built the house decided he wanted his privacy and a park, and diverted the road in a great sweep round the house and church, thus achieving his end with very little fuss. Once over the grid, which is meant to exclude rabbits, you approach the house from the back, through the orchard and part of the garden. The house, which is red brick and late Georgian, stands on a mini-terrace with a short flight of steps down to a large flat lawn about the size of six tennis courts. My husband could remember as a small boy following the old gardener, Harry, round and round the lawn while he was mowing, the mower dragged by a pony wearing special boots or shoes to avoid cutting the turf. Harry was still one of the two and a half gardeners there when we moved in. Both men had spent about fifty years in the garden; the old head gardener, who, sad to say, had retired, was head for fifty-four years.

When my father-in-law died, we pulled down two wings of the house. Where his sitting room used to be, we made a sunken paved garden. I thought some millstones would be decorative and visited a local, redundant mill. Unfortunately the miller dropped one of the stones on my foot. I was in plaster for six weeks, just before my daughter's wedding, but the mill owners were so contrite and concerned that they gave me the millstones, and they still look very decorative as steps up to a slightly higher level.

To break up the vast expanse of lawn, we planted a yew hedge at right angles to the house, with a border in front of it. It started by being herbaceous, divided in the centre with an elaborate old white wrought-iron seat, surrounded by white and silver plants merging to pale pinks and puces and blues towards each end. Now the border has a lot of shrub roses, such as *Rosa glauca* (syn. *R. rubrifolia*) and 'Lavender Lassie', and grey- and silver-leaved shrubs. It's such a pity that most grey, hardy, evergreen shrubs have yellow flowers. I like what I call dual-purpose shrubs and plants, which have some interest when not in flower or fruit and liven up the borders for the rest of the year with varying architectural shapes and contrasting foliage. For instance, I use a lot of 'full stop plants', such as phormium and yucca.

96 South front of the house with *Geranium psilostemon* and pink delphiniums, *Lychnis coronaria* 'Alba' with Rose 'Uncle Walter', which I bought in memory of my Uncle Walter, nephew of the old gardener Vicary Gibbs of Aldenham who died about 1929, in a year of deep recession. Although there was a lot of unemployment, my uncle, as Executor, found places for over 70 gardeners.

Beyond the lawn lies the park, with an avenue of trees leading into the distance; my son and daughter-in-law have recently made a ha-ha between the lawn and the park – a great improvement. A path running parallel to the house extends on either side for about 100 yards, with a thatched summer house at one end and a yew recess with a bronze horse's head sculpted by my daughter-in-law at the other.

On the other side of the lawn, opposite the yew hedge, stood an imposing chestnut tree. Sad to say, this fell down in a heap of dust and rotten wood, but it gave me the opportunity of making a shrub border with an excellent backdrop of yews and laurels, planted long ago on a mound to hide the church beyond. I put in a few good trees and shrubs and filled in with quick growers to be removed later. An *Acer negundo* 'Variegatum' has succumbed to honey fungus; I hope it doesn't spread. In one place we have sunk sheets of polythene at the path edge to discourage the fungus, and so far it has been successful. Rose 'Rambling Rector' was allowed, through neglect and unobservance, to take a wrong turn and rush up the acer, where he (or she) looked superb. He will now have to conform and join his fellows, such as 'Kiftsgate' and 'Brenda Colvin', climbing on to the yews behind.

Thanks to a suggestion by John Codrington, we cut down a yew to reveal the church tower and make a vista beyond a group of limes, with grass carefully trimmed to enhance and extend the view beyond the garden and on to the park.

Flanking the steps to the lawn and terrace, a retaining wall runs the length of the house. Under the wall we inherited a long border with a mass of old pink bush roses. No one knew their name, until I bought from Peter Beales some shrub roses that sounded just what I wanted and found I'd already got thirty of them! To these we have added clumps of nepeta, lavender and variegated iris.

To the south-east we made two new shrub borders, one of them to hide a hard tennis court. The pink Judas tree in one of these borders looks well against a large copper beech and flowers much better than the white one, which seems susceptible to birds eating the flowering buds. Also in the border is a *Viburnum davidii*; I was ignorant about its sex life and so had no blue berries. When I discovered this I bought two more, having explained my problem to the nursery-man. Still no berries, but they have grown over six feet high to compensate.

The soil is terrible, with a pH of about 8, and the

drainage poor, even though we put drains down the gentle slope on to the lawn. The rain seems to remain where it falls and, in the summer, the cracks in the earth are wide enough to put one's hand down; in the winter we stick in the borders and squelch on the grass. A cold wet wind prevails in spring and autumn and the north and east winds have nothing to moderate or warm them between Norfolk and the North Pole. Our rainfall is about 18 to 20 inches a year.

On the red brick walls, most south-facing, we try to keep the colours to yellows, blues, silver and white. *Buddleja auriculata* grew to twelve feet and left us twice without saying goodbye, although I gave them ample opportunity to reappear in the spring. *Erythrina crista-galli* said goodbye during two mild winters and good summers, gradually having fewer flowering stems. It was deciduous with me, but the three-foot stems of scarlet hooded flowers were spectacular in October for fifteen years. A *Wattakaka sinensis*, with its umbels of beautifully scented, hoya-like flowers, clambers up a tall 'Mermaid' rose. Everyone tells me it is not hardy but it has been unprotected and completely unmoved for the last twenty winters. In an unheated plastic tunnel in the nursery, its offspring were frozen in the winter of 1985/6 and all

the plants sprang into life and growth when warmer weather came. This is one of the plants I bought unseen from reading gardening books. It is unexpected, in that it has proved to be so much hardier than the ceanothus, *Solanum jasminoides* 'Album', *Buddleja auriculata* and *Nandina domestica*.

I planted snowdrops (*G. corcyrensis*) in front of our sitting-room windows under a big clump of Rose 'The Fairy', hoping that the rose leaves would fall off and we'd enjoy a drift of snowdrops in November and December. The rose then decided to become semi-evergreen until late December, but some years my plan has worked.

A *Cornus mas* at least ninety years old was blown over in the winter of 1984 because dull, protective evergreens had been removed. It was left for several months; when we did get round to clearing it up, I found about a quarter of the roots on one side were still more or less in the ground and the rest in the air, so

97 Edge of border along the drive. A large white wisteria covers the arch.

98 The portico, with a large *Magnolia* x *soulangiana* against the wall. The steps lead to the summerhouse past the rose garden.

99

100

101

102

we decided to put it back. We also cut it back drastically and it is now full of life and new growth and eight feet high.

We propagate a tremendous lot of shrubs and plants from the garden. I find my father-in-law's or perhaps grandfather-in-law's cut-throat razor wonderfully sharp and useful. We bought a rotovator to minimise digging. There used to be a negligible amount of oxalis in the kitchen garden; we realised too late that rotovating was obviously fatal, as it broke up the bulbs very nicely and every portion grew until, now, we have a complete, late summer ground cover. The weedkiller glyphosate helps but is not fatal. I have since refused to buy any variety of oxalis – I just do not trust the genus.

Gardens are always on the move and ours is constantly changing as we have better ideas – or think we have. To my mind a garden is never finished; there is always room for improvements and innovations, with plenty of scope to incorporate the ideas of future generations.

99 The old entrance to the house, where the drainage of the two raised borders is excellent as the whole enclosed garden is over the filled-in basement. *Allium schubertii* and many other plants have survived that do not in the rest of the garden. Rose 'Pompon de Paris' flowers profusely by the entrance; *Clematis rehderiana* and its lovely scented clusters of bell-shaped, pale yellow flowers cheers the left hand corner when the roses are over.

100 Davidia, (Handkerchief Tree, or the young call it Tissue Tree!) planted 20 years ago, which has flowered and seeded regularly for many years. Nearby are *Robinia* 'Frisia' in a fairly well-sheltered place, for they are very brittle, and *Acer ginnala* which gives excellent but fleeting autumn colour. It will have to have its head cut off to give the davidia more space.

101 *Cornus alternifolia* 'Argentea' with *Campanula lactiflora* 'Loddon Anna' and *Geranium endressii*, one of the many hardy geraniums used in any weed-free situation as ground cover. *Rosa glauca* and 'Constance Spry' are in the background.

102 *Rosa glauca*, pink delphiniums and lychnis in the border at right angles to the house.

103 Part of the 150-year old apple tree which can be traced back for over 100 years by two gardeners who each worked 50 years. The apple is a soft, green, early cooker.

The Hon. Mrs Charles Smith-Ryland's garden,
SHERBOURNE, WARWICKSHIRE

When we came to Sherbourne in 1953 there was little or no garden, just thirty-two rose beds and four clumps of pampas grass set in a flat lawn. The house, built about 1730–40, possibly by Smith of Warwick, is in a pretty red brick with stone quoins. We have offset the somewhat severe style by adding statues backed by curving wing brick walls and extending these with yew hedges. The house faces east but most of the planting has been done on the south side. The church of All Saints, built in 1863 by my husband's great-aunt to the design of Sir George Gilbert Scott, dominates both house and garden, and it is on its tall spire that I have concentrated some of the views. The fifth church on the site, Sherbourne was mentioned in the Domesday Book and takes its name from the old English Scirebourne, meaning 'clear water'. It is from this clear stream, running into the River Avon, that we have formed our lake.

The east front has a ha-ha separating it from the park, where I have planted clumps of trees, with specimen trees in the lawn to frame the view. *Acer pseudoplatanus* 'Brilliantissimum', *Castanea sativa* 'Albo-marginata,' *Koelreuteria paniculata, Betula utilis jacquemontii* and *Carpinus betulus* 'Fastigiata' are but a few. At the far end of this lawn and leading into the Wild Garden, is a little gazebo, the cast-iron, barley-sugar uprights rescued from a Victorian conservatory and surmounted by a modern wrought-iron dome.

One of the beauties of a garden is to find something different round every corner. To achieve this, I have tried to make contrasting vistas and separate enclosures. The main vista is centred on the south front of the house, going down the croquet lawn, across another, smaller ha-ha, and down a lime avenue over the River Avon to a clump of trees in the distance. Here imagination comes into play, as some of the trees are still very small!

I have tried to plant the borders in shades of complementary colours. Thus the croquet lawn is mainly in shades of buff, pink and mauve. Roses 'Cornelia', 'Penelope', 'William Lobb' and *Rosa primula* mingle with geraniums – 'Ballerina', *lancastriense* and 'Johnson's Blue'. *Abutilon vitifolium* 'Veronica Tennant', *Viburnum* x *bodnantense* 'Deben', *Exochorda* x *macrantha* 'The Bride', and many other shrubs terminate with *Crambe cordifolia*, which punctuates the corner in a cloud of white.

Sitting on the terrace surrounded by pots of scarlet bottle-brushes and apricot daturas, the evocative scents of *Magnolia grandiflora* 'Exmouth' and *Jasminum* x *stephanense* drift over one, soothing away the stresses of life and allowing the peace of the garden to take over. Here too the vivid yellow fremontodendron, coronilla, *Senecio italicus* and *Clematis tangutica* find a warm and sheltered spot with a lead peacock to preside over them.

The swimming pool, surrounded by brick walls and flower beds, is planted mainly for June onwards, but also for the spring with camellias and tulips. Here the darker and more brilliant colours of yellow and purple predominate. *Abutilon* x *suntense* 'Jermyns', *Humulus lupulus aureus*, roses 'Violette' and 'Reine

104 The steps up to the swimming pool are flanked by *Agapanthus campanulatus*, grown from seed collected in Kenya. The flowers of *Cytisus battandieri* complement the yellow leaves of the acacia and the border beyond.

des Violettes', *Clematis* 'Jackmanii Superba' and *C.* 'Ville de Lyon' grow with *Lonicera tragophylla* and *L.* x *brownii* 'Fuchsioides' above borders of nerines, crinums and agapanthus. A *Campsis grandiflora*, *Trachelospermum jasminoides*, *Jasminum officinale* and a white *Solanum jasminoides* cover the swimming pool hut and are later-flowering.

Stone steps lead down to the bottom lawn, where a crossing axis of *Sorbus hupehensis* and *S.* 'Joseph Rock' divide the lawn into quarters with focal points at the end of each vista. A terracotta eagle dominates the south-facing yellow, blue and white border, while the other avenue is continued with *Pyrus salicifolia* 'Pendula', planted for our silver wedding, and ending with a grey stone sculpture of putti.

At the far end, under the churchyard wall and partially hidden by a large gean, is a little Box Garden; the pattern has been cribbed and simplified from the one in my grandmother's garden in Suffolk. Here the garden surrounds the churchyard and the mellow brick walls make a marvellous background for *Ceanothus* 'Topaz', rose 'New Dawn', *Lonicera periclymenum* 'Serotina'. A goldfish pond is surmounted by a *bas-relief* of Warwickshire's emblem, The Bear and Ragged Staff, which came from Warwick Castle.

The White Garden is surrounded by high yew hedges – tall and thin, they bear witness to good cutting over the years. They enclose triangular-shaped beds which form a diamond pattern punctuated by eight *Juniperus* 'Skyrocket'. It is a peaceful place to sit and one where I often linger. Sheltered from the winds, *Carpenteria californica*, *Abutilon vitifolium album*, *Fabiana imbricata*, *Hoheria lyallii* and *Olearia* x *scilloniensis* flower well. The shrubs are surrounded to overflowing by perennial plants, including delphiniums, lupins, the double form of *Sanguinaria canadensis*, *Cistus laurifolius* and *C.* x *corbariensis*, *Geranium pratense album* and *G. clarkei* 'Kashmir White'. The white chaenomeles, jasmine, roses and clematis clothe the walls, and white perennial sweet peas mixed with honeysuckles clamber over the wrought-iron archways.

Leaving this enclosed and rather quiet place, one comes to the latest (and, my husband hopes, final) extension of the garden, which is a small arboretum planted round the lake, which we dug in 1975. On the mound opposite we have placed a small temple to catch the eye and to tempt you further. It is from this viewpoint that the church, with its tall nineteenth-century Gothic spire, dominates the scene and is re-

107

108

flected in the water which surrounds it on two sides. After eight years of planting, the trees are beginning to make an impact. A *Cedrus deodara*, a paulownia, *Catalpa bignonioides*, several sorbus species and *Populus lasiocarpa* are mixed with acers, gleditsia and prunus. *P. virginiana* 'Shubert', whose leaves turn from green to purple as the season progresses, is one of my favourites. The lake is a lovely addition and makes a walk of constant pleasure, with the bubbling noise of the Sherbourne brook in the background.

Returning once more to the main garden, the south walk is planted in shades of pink and blue. A fine white wisteria climbs through *Prunus cerasifera* 'Pissardii', and *Indigofera heterantha* (*I. gerardiana*) and *I. potaninii* are pretty in late summer. Further on, a group of silver pear, *Acer palmatum* 'Atropurpureum' and *Ribes odoratum* is particularly effective.

The old kitchen garden is now filled with greenhouses and here the talented Rodney Dedey propagates and sells shrubs from the garden.

I love every facet of the garden, warts, disasters and all. It has grown up with me and, having placed every stick and stone, I know it like an old friend. I am fascinated by the shapes and colours of plants and often carry a new arrival round the garden to place it

exactly. I think I became a plant snob the day a friend said I had a lot of common plants. Since then I have collected and culled and enjoyed every moment of it. Walking round the garden with friends is one of life's greater pleasures and one realises how lucky one is to live in such a place and to derive such happiness from it.

J. Smith Ryland

105 The Shepherd Boy, one of a pair, his feet surrounded by bergenias, *Euphorbia characias wulfenii* and *Fuchsia* 'Thalia', his head wreathed in clematis and honeysuckle, guards the entrance to the gardens.

106 A terracotta eagle looks down from his plinth beneath a *Robinia pseudacacia* 'Frisea'. Glimpsed between *Potentilla* 'Elizabeth' and *Erysimum linifolium*, he is the focal point of an avenue of *Sorbus hupehensis* and 'Joseph Rock'.

107 The Box Garden has standard wisterias planted with Rose 'Anna' and 'Pinkie'. Standard honeysuckles are underplanted with various lavenders and grey-leaved plants.

108 Rose 'Ednaston Climber' smothers an old pear tree on the churchyard wall.

Mrs Thomas Gibson's garden, BURFORD, OXFORDSHIRE

Our love affair with the garden at Westwell began the moment we saw it in 1979. The garden, rather than the house, made us feel we must have it. Cotswold stone walls and mature yew and box hedges divided the garden into compartments, and we explored from one enclosure to the next with mounting delight and excitement.

We were newcomers to a garden that had been laid out and cared for by the Holland family for the major part of the twentieth century. A short interregnum immediately before our arrival had produced some unwelcome additions (one hundred and twenty Leyland cypresses, orange Hybrid Tea roses) but we were taking on an established garden with fine eighteenth-century walls and gates, topiary and hedges, and low walls and paving dating from the early 1900s.

Our first winter was spent in a fever of plans and plant catalogues and an immersion in garden books from Parkinson to Dame Sylvia Crowe. Head reeling with advice, I would step out into the garden in a daze, to be soothed by some new discovery. Each week brought a fresh delight: an unusual shrub, a succession of bulbs, starting with a carpet of aconites under the huge hanging chestnuts at the front of the house and ending with a triumph of narcissi in the small orchard.

Despite advice to the contrary, we could not resist the temptation to start before a year was up, and the first step was to remove the Hybrid Tea roses from the rose garden, banishing the more lurid ones completely and planting the rest in the cutting garden. The eight

109 The herbaceous border in its bridal, late June dress with *Crambe cordifolia* and sweet rocket predominating among astrantia and angelica. At this time of year, the colours in the border are predominantly white, mauve and green.

rose beds were then each filled with a different variety of Gallica, Alba or Bourbon rose, 'Madame Isaac Pereire' for her delectable scent, Rosa Mundi for its fascinating parti-coloured petals and wealth of historical associations. Keeping to white, pink and crimson, it was hard to limit the choice to eight. These were underplanted with a deep crimson-flowered origanum brought from our last garden, parahebe and *Geranium* 'Wargrave Pink'. The Leyland cypresses were disposed of and a group of balsam poplars planted by the pond on the eastern boundary of the garden, so that in spring and autumn the air is filled with their entrancing scent. We widened the grass path between the two main herbaceous borders and laid down a mowing stone so that the plants could billow out without ruining the grass. In all this David Baldwin, who has worked here since he was fifteen, was the mainstay; his unfailing good nature, as one scheme after another was sprung on him, has contributed enormously to our pleasure in the garden. He has since been joined part-time by Roy Holtom, who brought a wealth of experience with him after thirty-two years at the lovely Bampton Manor gardens. At any one time they have up to three thousand cuttings in the greenhouse and cold frames, ready to fill any gap or take part in a new plan.

Gardening cannot really be called a family activity; nevertheless there are times when I have dragooned my husband and sons into participation. Thomas is a very useful six foot three inches, so that, standing with his arms raised above his head, he can do a fair imitation of a standard ex-nursery tree. Callers might be surprised to see him planted in a newly acquired urn, bending and straightening his knees obligingly as

110

111

I gallop from viewpoint to viewpoint, trying to decide whether a standard or a half standard tree would be more suitable.

Our sons have a far firmer grip on mental arithmetic than I do and all have done stalwart work at the end of a tape measure, answering such thorny problems as, 'If I have a space sixty-seven and a half feet long, and I want to plant trees at seven-foot intervals, allowing for one gap of ten feet for a path, how many trees do I need?' This almost compensates for my indignation when they drive a mini motorized tricycle over the grass verges, or the impotent fury I feel when I spot a cricket ball hurtling towards a prized *Eremurus robustus* in the herbaceous border. It is easy to see why gardening is so often an enthusiasm not fully realised until middle age. Having reached that enviable plateau, it is a relief to be free from the tyranny of the sand-pit.

Westwell is very much an enclosed, inward-looking garden, Tudor in feeling. We learnt to our cost the folly of not obeying Pope's famous dictum to consult the *genius loci* when we bought four marble statues of the Seasons. Very pretty in themselves and in the shop, but when (with great difficulty, owing to their immense weight) we got them to their chosen places in the garden, they looked stridently neo-classical and

112

110 Two matching double rectangles of *Carpinus betulus* were planted in two vacant stretches of gently sloping lawn. A Greek oil jar is placed in the centre of each with inverted, sunken staddle-stones leading to it and providing a pleasing contrast of texture with the grass.

111 A newly planted short avenue of *Pyrus calleryana* 'Chanticleer' stands above the old yew hedge and topiary and is here seen across a mass of pink Japanese anemones which follow on after the paeonies in the lily pond beds and seed themselves with pleasing prodigality.

112 A corner of the predominantly white garden where a new mowing stone was laid in 1981 to allow the plants to burst from their beds without marring the grass. Here the gold edges of *Melissa variegata* 'Aurea' complement the varied whites of *Lilium regale*, delphinium, anaphalis, *Hebe* 'Pagei' and Rose 'Blanc Double de Coubert'.

113 The newly planted outdoor dining room is made up of a circle of *Alnus glutinosa* with three white cherries and three white thorns amongst them, to be woven into an informal basket as they mature. The setting is the meadow garden where wild flowers are being encouraged to follow on after a carpet of narcissi.

113

disastrously out of place. A few weeks later they were trundled expensively away.

Not for us the expansive views and confident ownership of the eighteenth century, but rather a return to an earlier age when the garden was a secret, protected place with patterns of trees, arches through hedges and the eye permanently kept inside the boundary wall which shut out a hostile world. No wavy-edged island beds with colourful shrubs or bedding out plants, but formal symmetrical lines softened by a profusion of flowers in controlled colour ranges. This has been the thinking behind the additions we have made.

There is something inexplicably fascinating about trees arranged in avenues, rows and grids. I find that they never fail to excite and satisfy. Our first venture in this area was a short avenue of pleached limes either side of the drive at the front of the house. I could find no instructions on exactly how to pleach a tree in any of our gardening books, so we used common sense

114 The pergola which leads from the rose garden is planted with roses 'Climbing Iceberg' and 'Mme Alfred Carrière', which here frame the budding *Lilium regale* below them and a bank of nepeta beyond. The area is surrounded on three sides by mature yew hedges.

and native cunning. Unsuspecting friends staying for the weekend found themselves poised dangerously at the top of ladders, hammering long, heavy stakes into the ground while the home team accomplished the less taxing task of placing the trees and standing back to criticise or admire the effect.

Flushed with enthusiasm, we have gone on to plant a row of *Malus* 'John Downie' along the back drive, a grid of *Robinia pseudacacia* 'Inermis' in the small orchard and a short avenue of *Pyrus calleryana* 'Chanticleer', which obligingly holds its leaves right into February. We have also enclosed two rectangular areas in matching stretches of lawn with double rows of hornbeams, to be clipped into a hedge on legs. These have the dual purpose of breaking up a rather too large sloping area of grass, forming a comfortable room, and, with the inclusion of an old Greek oil jar at each centre, providing a focal point from several windows in the house. Unfortunately, despite attentive watering, feeding and mulching, the trees do not flourish. We have replaced several of them and they continue to survive but not to enjoy life. This is a constant source of disappointment in gardening for, however carefully one plots and plants, if the thing does not take off and look happy, at least half the pleasure is lost.

Similar troubles in the rose garden forced us to take drastic action and, on Penelope Hobhouse's advice, we lifted all the roses and underplanting and treated the beds with Basamid last October in an attempt to banish rose replant disease and re-invigorate the soil. This involved covering the beds with polythene sheets for eight weeks and we wait anxiously to see if the cure has worked.

The soil here is very light, limey and stony. We are mulching and fertilising systematically, so hope for better results throughout soon, but I am not counting on it. Mother Nature has a very sure way of confirming one's ignorance and her own superiority.

The twin herbaceous borders divided by a grass path are a constant challenge. I made the mistake of planting groups that were too small and looked bitty in such a large area. Now we are trying to plant in large, bold drifts of fifteen or more plants in many cases and to introduce fleshy and waxy leaves in summer to counteract the dried-hayfield look. To this end *Galtonia candicans* and *G. princeps* have been used as well as *Gladiolus callianthus* (*Acidanthera murielae*) and glaucous-leaved hostas. The colours shift throughout the seasons, starting with soft mauves and pinks and whites and ending, in October, with a blaze of golden achillea and rich purple Michaelmas daisies. There is always something wrong and I write myself numerous notes and stick labels in to remind us of changes for next year. I have learnt from regular visits to RHS shows at Vincent Square and from visiting other gardens whenever possible. I have filled several notebooks with names of plants and instructions to myself, but it will take a lifetime to carry them all out.

Some flowers are so striking that they are underscored and labelled MUST. Such a one was Beth Chatto's *Sisyrinchium striatum* 'Aunt May', which survived only a year but gave great pleasure while it did and is still mourned. Another was the very good-natured *Tricyrtis stolonifera*, whose speckled petals give it an unaccountable fascination. I love speckled or strangely coloured flowers and we have planted *Fritillaria pontica* and *F. acmopetala* round *Pyrus salicifolia* 'Pendula' in square beds edged with santolina. The bulbs are so expensive that they need to be in a safely enclosed spot to be sure they are not lost. Their more common but equally beautiful cousin, the *Fritillaria meleagris*, grows in drifts in the rough grass at the front of the house. We have some *Primula auricula* in stone troughs on a low wall and hope to add the charming grey and white flowered one if the seeds come up true to their parent.

In one area of the garden immediately to the south and east of the house we have limited the planting to white and mauve flowers, with a dominance of silver foliage. *Convolvulus cneorum*, *Teucrium fruticans*, *Lilium regale*, Rose 'Blanc Double de Coubert', cream-flowered santolina, *Iris pallida* 'Variegata', *Hosta sieboldiana* and various artemisias form the backbone and lend the garden a slightly ghostly look, particularly by moonlight, a rather neglected time which gives a garden a whole new dimension.

In another part of the garden we have set purple sage interplanted with *Allium christophii* (*A. albopilosum*), to be followed by *Aster* x *frikartii*, against a wall hung with *Ceanothus impressus* 'Puget Blue' and *Clematis* 'Perle d'Azur'. In the Bunny Walk, a long, narrow grassed area enclosed by a high box hedge on one side and a south-facing wall on the other, we have concentrated on pinks of all shades, from the dusky pink of *Salvia officinalis* 'Tricolor' to the bright pinks of annual cosmos and the deep tones of Rose 'Zéphirine Drouhin'. Foxgloves and lavatera add silvery foliage which seems to go well.

Our latest project is to turn our productive but ugly vegetable garden into an earthly paradise, aiming for an English look, with brick paths, box edging, fruit arches, standard gooseberries and miniature espalier pears, rather than the grand open formalities of a French potager. Progress has been halted by the coldest February for forty years, but my head is full of pictures of how I hope it will look and I am watching the barometer impatiently for signs of thaw. If only all one's visions would materialise, the garden would indeed be a miraculous place. As it is, the job is to work to narrow the gap between vision and reality, and in this I am always learning from friends, experts, books and a dictum still not fully absorbed: at all times use your eyes.

Anthea Gibson

Mrs Anne Stevens' garden, ANSTY, DORSET

When I moved to Ivy Cottage in 1964, I knew it was just the type of garden I had dreamed of. Although it was then overgrown with tall nettles, docks and horse-tails under half-dead old willows, hazels and sapling elms, and only one third of the garden was under cultivation, the land sloped gently down to a delightful little stream where the slightly acid soil was suitable for growing all the moisture-loving plants which I liked. In other parts of the garden I was lucky to have deep, rich, easily worked loam. Over the next few years, helped by my husband, I was able gradually to reclaim the overgrown parts of the garden, enlarging the borders and making new beds. I began my planting programme with specimen trees and shrubs, followed by hundreds of bulbs and perennials.

Now, in front of the thatched cottage, large her-baceous borders on either side of the main lawn slope gracefully down towards the stream. These borders are crammed with hundreds of perennials, including many bulbous ones; they create a marvellous display of colour, beginning in early spring and continuing well into autumn. *Ajuga* 'Burgundy Glow' and *A.* 'Rainbow' form dense, low mats of attractive foliage in the front, together with golden thyme, *Pulmonaria rubra* 'Redstart', *Iris innominata*, *Primula sibthorpii* and several varieties of hosta. The well-established clumps of *Hosta* 'Halcyon', with its lovely blue-grey leaves, are always much admired by visitors, as are the clumps of *H. fortunei* 'Albopicta', which is one of my

favourites for its outstanding foliage in May and June – bright yellow, eye-catching leaves thinly edged with green – followed by lilac, lily-shaped flowers in July, and the leaves gradually fading to a soft green in late summer.

In the middle of the border I have planted *Euphorbia polychroma*, *Geranium* x *magnificum* and *G. psilostemon*, *Alstroemeria ligtu* hybrids, several varieties of oriental poppy, and *Stachys macrantha*, which has dense heads of mauve flowers and good dark-green, serrated-edged leaves. I think this plant should be more widely grown. The day lilies, or *Hemerocallis*, provide bold splashes of colour in the summer. *H. middendorfiana*, with fragrant yellow blooms, is one of the earliest to flower, in early June. The bright reddy-bronze blooms of *H.* 'Tejas', such a reliable variety, flower in July. In midsummer, at the back of the border, the fine white plumes of *Aruncus dioicus* associate well with tall delphiniums, *Echinops ritro* and the scarlet *Lychnis chalcedonica*, the Maltese Cross Flower. For good autumn colour I have planted *Aster acris* and *A.* 'Carnival', a cherry-red variety 18 inches tall (both of these Michaelmas daisies are mildew-resistant), Japanese anemones, solidaster, *Physostegia virginiana* 'Vivid' and the unusual *Salvia involucrata* 'Bethellii' which has bright pink bracts covering the flower buds. Many of the spaces between the perennials are filled with bulbs of all kinds: snow-drops, crocus and narcissi for spring, and alliums, camassias and lilies for summer. In any other empty spaces I scatter seeds of annuals, using love-in-a-mist, candytuft and a shaggy poppy called 'Pink Chiffon' to great effect.

Leaving the borders behind, one can stroll down the

115 Massed moisture-loving *Primula* 'Bartley Strain' and *P. pulverulenta* growing at the end of the Ditch Garden in late May. Marsh marigolds, *Caltha palustris*, grow at the base of a hazel. In the background, fragrant yellow azaleas and a young specimen *Metasequoia glyptostroboides*.

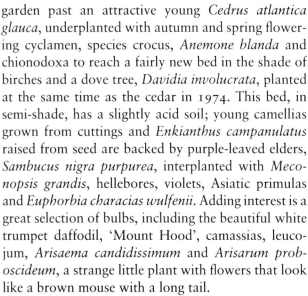

garden past an attractive young *Cedrus atlantica glauca*, underplanted with autumn and spring flowering cyclamen, species crocus, *Anemone blanda* and chionodoxa to reach a fairly new bed in the shade of birches and a dove tree, *Davidia involucrata*, planted at the same time as the cedar in 1974. This bed, in semi-shade, has a slightly acid soil; young camellias grown from cuttings and *Enkianthus campanulatus* raised from seed are backed by purple-leaved elders, *Sambucus nigra purpurea*, interplanted with *Meconopsis grandis*, hellebores, violets, Asiatic primulas and *Euphorbia characias wulfenii*. Adding interest is a great selection of bulbs, including the beautiful white trumpet daffodil, 'Mount Hood', camassias, leucojum, *Arisaema candidissimum* and *Arisarum proboscideum*, a strange little plant with flowers that look like a brown mouse with a long tail.

A small wooden bridge crosses the stream and, from there, you can walk into the kitchen garden, which is surrounded by a *Lonicera nitida* hedge. I enjoy growing vegetables, perhaps because I enjoy even more being able to pick and eat them fresh from the garden. I do all the work in the kitchen garden myself, even the digging. I really like digging, especially on a crisp day in autumn.

Adjoining the vegetable plots is a large fruit cage, with gooseberries, strawberries, raspberries and red, white and black currants. We had to put wire netting round the bottom and bury six inches of it in the ground in order to keep out the badgers, which are a huge problem and would eat all the strawberries and raspberries if given half a chance. They are forever digging up the lawn, looking for worms and leatherjackets to eat and, if they are very hungry, will chew carrots and beetroots.

Near the kitchen garden a large, roughly triangular bed is filled with moisture-loving plants, including lovely Candelabra primulas, astilbe, trollius, rheum and *Rodgersia podophylla* – a striking plant in spring and early summer when the young leaves are a bronze colour. The NCCPG's (National Council for the Conservation of Plants and Gardens) national collection of trollius is housed here at Ivy Cottage – our rich, moist soil suits them, and I am always trying to locate species and varieties I do not already have.

A wide grassy path winds through the woodland area of the garden, where ashes and poplars eighty feet tall provide a canopy for azaleas and rhododendrons, and hollies give some protection from the cold north winds. Daffodils and narcissi are naturalised here and with primroses and marsh marigolds give a marvellous display in spring. I am hoping to establish groups of erythroniums, *Trillium sessile* and *Cardiocrinum giganteum*, as they should enjoy this cool woodland setting.

Along the narrow, wet banks of the Ditch Garden at the back of the cottage grow stately *Iris sibirica*, with *Filipendula rubra* and *Ligularia przewalskii* 'The Rocket' – a handsome plant with tall spikes of tiny starry yellow flowers on tall dark brown stems with large, heart-shaped, serrated-edged leaves. Maroon-purple *Primula pulverulenta* and bright pink *Primula* 'Bartley Strain' are massed at one end of the ditch. Marsh marigolds grow in the water and also *Lysichitom americanum*, whose large yellow arum-like flowers appear before the huge oval leaves. *Gunnera manicata* dwarf other plants with enormous leaves on stout and bristly seven-foot stems; it thrives in a spectacular manner in very moist soils but dies down completely during the winter.

The sloping ground around the Ditch Garden is filled with conifers, deciduous trees and shrubs. In 1977 we planted *Picea breweriana*, a beautiful, slow-growing, weeping conifer, as well as *Araucaria araucana* and an *Abies grandis*. Through the trees the bright yellow, young leaves of *Philadelphus coronarius* 'Aureus' show up well, together with *Viburnum plicatum* 'Mariesii' and *Itea ilicifolia*, an evergreen shrub with long drooping racemes of greenish little flowers in late summer. In this area over the years I have tried several of the old varieties of shrub roses, but without much success, as they do not like the rather humid atmosphere.

The driest and highest part of the garden is on the right of the drive, where there is a border, backed by a six-foot beech hedge, ideal conditions for *Penstemon* 'Charles Rudd', whose lilac flowers will keep blooming well into autumn or until the first hard frost. *Penstemon glaber* is also hardy, but much smaller, and throughout the summer will produce many spikes of small tubular blue flowers that fade to mauvy-pink with age. In the same border I grow *Salvia leucantha*; the white flowers are produced on gracefully arching stems and look more attractive when in bud, as they are covered by woolly violet calyces. This salvia is only hardy in the mildest of winters, and I always take some cuttings in autumn to overwinter in my conservatory. *Pulsatilla vulgaris*, *Acaena* 'Blue Haze' – such a good, silver foliage carpeting plant – and violas grow in the front of this dry border, mixed with *Allium cernuum*,

118

A. pulchellum and the superb *A. christophii*, with large, ball-shaped heads of tiny mauve, starry flowers. I collect alliums and now have over thirty varieties.

Anne Stevens

116 A section of vegetable garden in early summer with all the young plants growing well. In the foreground, lettuce 'Tom Thumb'; behind, young cabbage ready for transplanting, beetroot 'Detroit', lettuce 'Little Gem' and peas 'Hurst Green Shaft'.

117 One of the herbaceous borders in early autumn with still plenty of colour to be seen. At the back, *Crocosmia paniculata* grows to 5 feet. Other tall plants include Japanese anemones 'White Queen' and the lovely pink 'Queen Charlotte'. Also pictured are solidago, *Physostegia virginiana* 'Vivid', *Aster acris* and *Sedum* 'Autumn Joy'.

118 Branches of a mature weeping willow hang gracefully over the pond, providing convenient perches for the kingfishers which sometimes visit the garden. The large leaves of *Gunnera manicata* shade *Primula* 'Postford White'. Across the pond, *Menyanthes trifoliata*, the bog bean, grows out over the water.

Mrs Joyce Robinson's garden, FONTWELL, SUSSEX

You ask me what we have done at Denmans since you were here last. The answer is, 'A lot!' I should like you to see it. We came here in 1946, when it was difficult to get building materials. We needed to restore the gardener's cottage and make it our home; eventually we did, along with the other cottages and buildings.

At the same time we were clearing the garden and farm too; they had not been used for nearly ten years, and everything needed attention. I shall never forget that first summer with the fields yellow with ragwort, weeds waist-high in the garden and a continuous bonfire. There were two privet hedges, which we quickly removed, but also some lovely old apple trees which are still standing. In the park by the house the cedar of Lebanon towered above us all, as it still does, and there are lovely lime trees, sweet chestnuts and evergreen oaks which have stood well. The larger beeches (planted about 1850) were in bad shape though, and many were broken and had to be felled. We planted the nuts and the thuja hedge by the lane, which, with some Lawsons, eucalyptus, pittosporum and *Cupressus arizonica*, has made a good windbreak.

For the first five years we grew things for the London market: scabious, *Lilium regale*, Dutch iris and tons of strawberries. We missed the cattle which we had had at our previous home, so I reared a few heifer calves,

and we built up a herd of fifty Guernseys and kept forty sows. With their manure, the soil was restored to good heart for the garden I was eager to make, though I had no thoughts of having one so large – like Topsy, it 'just growed'. People often ask me if I had a plan but, since I had had no professional training, I just *made* the garden.

It is on a well-drained, gentle, southern slope of slightly alkaline loam over gravel. In 1952, I started to think further ahead and planted small trees and flowering shrubs, making a setting for borders with small lawns between. Throughout run areas of water-worn gravel, in which masses of biennials, small shrublets and perennials form year-round, colourful ground cover. Here are the hellebores *H. corsicus* and *H. foetidus*, both good in leaf and flower. There are no straight lines or corners, so the whole garden gently curves down to the water garden, which looks particularly good in the autumn with water lilies and a lot of fish and dragonflies.

The walled garden, in which were once soft fruit cages, was a mass of broken wire netting and iron posts. We grew vegetables and sometimes early strawberries there until 1970, when I decided that we were working too hard, so it was ploughed – paths and all. Here was a challenge! Should it be water and statuary, fruit or just plants? It had everything: the shelter of eight-foot-high flint walls; it was south-facing, well drained and slightly sloping. What more could I wish? It should, I decided, be a mass of plants and climbers.

After ploughing, I made my first mistake: the wall border facing west – the most favourable for tender things – should have been at least ten feet deep. Depth is so much more important than length in any border.

119 Herbs in the walled garden, set in gravel and paving stones: a rich planting of purple, grey and gold including Rugosa 'Scabrosa', lavenders, *Digitalis* x *mertonensis* and *D. grandiflora*, *Lonicera* 'Baggesen's Gold', a tall *Verbascum bombyciferum* and *Salvia sclarea turkestanica* and *S. aurea*. The flint wall is covered with *Clematis montana* 'Rubens', complimented by golden feverfew and giant chives in the gravel.

All is now furnished with climbers and wall plants: roses, clematis, wisteria, tecoma, honeysuckle, feijoa, myrtles, pomegranate, magnolias and solanums, some reaching up and over the wall to the other side. The paths are wide and merge into wider areas of gravel in which everything seeds, so the whole garden and walls are filled with glorious disarray. For shape and height a few shrub roses, daphnes, hebes, a purple berberis, a eucalyptus and a *Robinia pseudacacia* 'Frisia' grow through each other, making the whole my very own enchanted garden.

When I went to the Greek islands, I noticed how everything grew so well in gravel and stones, but it was in Delos that I had the inspiration to make the gravel garden which I have so much enjoyed. With the tractor I drew what I hoped would describe dry stream beds and a dry water-hole. The streams are some eight feet wide and only a few inches deep, curving down across the lawn for about 100 hundred yards to the water-hole. I placed large pieces of local sandstone rocks at intervals, then covered it all with gravel from the sea bed. A wide piece of natural stone forms a foot-bridge, and I have planted only things that would grow naturally in a dry watercourse. It was finished some years before the water garden, which is at the bottom of the slope and now completes the picture.

There was an early planting of silver birches and ornamental cherries, which are now large trees and shelter the more tender things I have been given by

120 Yellow lilies on the pool. On the far bank, a spring picture of *Hosta sieboldiana* 'Elegans', *Iris pallida* 'Variegata', orange Candelabra primulas, leaves of *Ligularia* 'The Rocket' and comfrey – all reflected in the water. The giant hogweed is just showing, with a purple phormium behind.

121 Where the dry stream meets the pool, there is a planting of different tree shapes. The silver foliage and white trunks of a group of eucalyptus shine against the more sober *Liriodendron tulipifera* and *Cupressus macrocarpa* 'Goldcrest'. In the foreground, a young snakebark maple, *Acer davidii*, with some field maples and yellow iris. Through the eucalyptus branches can be seen a horse chestnut in flower.

122 Climbing R. 'Bleu Magenta' clothes the wall and an entrance into the walled garden, where its soft purple clusters of scented flowers need partial shade.

123 *Rheum palmatum* 'Bowles Crimson', with large crinkled red leaves, under an apricot tree in the walled garden. Tucked in behind is *Euonymus* 'Emerald 'n' Gold', with feverfew in the gravel. In the background, *Euphorbia robbiae* and, on the wall, an old Bourbon rose 'Mme Isaac Pereire'.

122

123

124

specialist growers. Some plants have come from Kew and Wisley. We have arbutus, liquidambar, some magnolias, *Parrotia persica*, *Acer palmatum* 'Sango Kaku', *A. japonicum* 'Aureum', *A. griseum* and the snake-bark *A. davidii* plus the grey-leaved *Pyrus salicifolia* 'Pendula', the Colorado white spruce, eucalyptus, feijoa, *Rhamnus alaternus* 'Argenteovariegata' and many other grey shrubby things that mix so well.

We are lucky to have the old flint walls round most of the garden, and have clothed them and the buildings with climbers and wall plants and a lot of roses. 'Wedding Day' has grown out through the top of an old russet apple, and touches the ground. I can never have enough roses, but I do like them grown as shrubs and planted with other things, and on their own roots. We grow mostly the species and 'old-fashioned' ones – the Rugosas and old China roses, *R. moyesii* and its seedlings, *R. chinensis*, and *R. californica* and *R. xanthina* 'Canary Bird' – there are so many! We grow them among herbs and flowering shrubs, in borders – in fact, everywhere. Clematis like to be grown with other things too, and are happy rambling over shrubs. *Clematis rehderiana*, *C. tibetana* ssp. *vernayi* and *C.* 'Huldine' are at their best in mid-September, when *C. armandii* has had a second blooming.

I made a purple planting last autumn with which I am delighted; a real mixture, with a lot of pink penstemons, dierama, phlox, arctotis and the purple and variegated ajuga. For the autumn there are kaffir lilies and *Kniphofia caulescens*, *Hosta plantaginea* and large clumps of Japanese anemones, which flower right through to October.

One of my interests has been collecting winter plants and shrubs of beauty and scent. Anyone can have a garden in the spring, but nothing gives more joy than gathering a bowl of flowers from your garden at Christmas time. Winter sweet and witch hazel, the winter-flowering honeysuckles, *Cornus mas*, the viburnums, abeliophyllum – all on bare winter stems and all sweetly scented, especially when brought into a warm room.

Making large patches of interest among the variegated hollies and other grey and golden evergreens, the green-flowered hellebores and the long catkins of *Garrya elliptica* look wonderful in January. These early treasures never fail to surprise me.

The conservatory, although still in fair condition after almost a hundred years, is our only heated area. I have planted it profusely with fairly easy things, and it is overflowing with *Cassia corymbosa*, periploca,

sollya (the bluebell creeper from Australia), the small strawberry guava, herbertia, *Clematis* 'Comtesse de Bouchaud', and much else. In the ground, in gravel and flagstones, are arums, agapanthus, clivias, ferns, eucalyptus, tibouchina and a climbing rose. Everything grows on the benches and in large containers — geraniums, fuchsias, grey and gold helichrysum, hyacinths and other bulbs. There is never enough room for over-wintering all our tender things.

The large unheated frame house, where we grew commercial crops, is now roof-high with New Zealand and other half-hardy plants that appreciate wind shelter. We grow there *Acacia pravissima*, callistemons, passiflora, myrtles, phormiums, plumbago, jasmines and clematis. In about a quarter of the house we grow salad crops in the summer and in the winter hold plants in containers and potted-up cuttings for replacements and for sale to garden visitors.

Have I answered your question? I rather think I have been carried away! But apart from the family, my whole life is plants and gardens. Now, after forty years of making the garden, I have retired, and since Christmas 1984 John Brookes is caring for it, so Denmans will go forward as a teaching garden. It is well to know it is in such good hands.

124 'The Dreamer', by Marion Smith, gazes across the lily pool among bullrushes, *Sambucus nigra* 'Marginata' and *Viburnum plicatum* 'Lanarth'. He is well sheltered by arundinarias, contoneasters, *variegated japonicus* and some conifers.

125 *Viburnum plicatum* 'Mariesii' in full bloom. Through it can be seen the tall, pointed leaves of *Phormium tenax* 'Variegatum'. In front, a young *Acer griseum* with its paper-like bark and showing a cinnamon coloured under-bark. In autumn, the leaves turn a wonderful fiery colour, even on small trees.

Mrs John Makepeace's garden, BEAMINSTER, DORSET

My garden surrounds a lovely Tudor manor, built of mellow hamstone in a wooded valley, with a small river marking its long western boundary. Parnham, empty and neglected for several years, was bought by my husband in 1976, as a home and as a business and school devoted to fine twentieth-century furniture-making. Fourteen acres is all that remains of extensive estates and rolling parkland once belonging to this house. The garden has many sheltered aspects, but it is in a frost pocket and suffers from howling south-west winds funnelling up the valley from the sea, six miles away.

A turning point in Parnham's history came in 1910, when a wealthy and far-sighted owner had much of the garden landscaped – speculation points to Inigo Thomas or Harold Peto as likely landscape architects. The work included an elegant walled forecourt and the creation of three grand terraces. The first, wrapping around the south front, is balustraded and punctuated by twin gazebos overlooking fifty wonderful conically clipped yew trees forming two squares intersected by water rills and cascades. The lowest terrace is divided from the old parkland by a ha-ha wall; more balustrading marks the end of the garden, where once there was a lake. This southerly area is so beautiful it needed little to bring it back to perfection. We have planted lots of trees here, as elsewhere, and roses against the many walls. But everywhere north of the house — including enclosed gardens, courtyards, walkways, an eighty-yard-long Italian Garden and a woodland of an acre or so – these became the palette on to which I had

126 The climbing rose 'Goldbusch' on one of the stone pillars at the entrance to the front forecourt. 'Constance Spry' grows as a pillar rose on the right.

the daunting task of bringing years of indifference to life.

My enthusiasm for gardening had always been strong, influenced by my mother who created lovely gardens in various childhood homes, but until Parnham I had had no sense of responsibility. Since we are open to the public twice a week, it was essential to create a garden both pleasing and challenging. Many of the dark winter evenings are spent with my books, learning, planning and just enjoying. Christopher Lloyd, with his sharp wit and honest criticism, has been a fund of sound advice. H. E. Bates, better known for his novels, wrote two lovely books which are a great inspiration; the work of Graham Stuart Thomas, of the late Sybil Emberton, of Penelope Hobhouse, Wisley's excellent technical manuals and a super little book called *Plant Names Simplified* (Latin for ignoramuses) are some of the sources to which I constantly refer. I rarely have time to visit other gardens but, of those I have seen, Dartington, which I often visit, is a great favourite. It was there that I first saw bog primulas growing in abundance; and great drifts of crocus below the beeches; and exotic climbers – especially *Akebia quinata* – in the sheltered old courtyard, all of which have found homes at Parnham.

Luckily, three years ago I discovered Leslie Sewell, our only full-time gardener. (I am sad to say he retired from Parnham in 1986.) Our ideas were originally fairly disparate, but I stubbornly resisted all temptation to provide instant colour with annual bedding, persuading Leslie that it was inappropriate here where permanent planting provides more interest and less work. Leslie filled all the big stone tubs on the terraces and other focal points with a wonderful selection of fuchsias, geraniums, *Helichrysum petiolatum* and lobelias, all grown from seeds and cuttings in his tiny greenhouse. He did all the mowing – about eight acres a week – the hedge trimming and topiary and much of the general maintenance. I did all of the planning, most of the planting and pruning and much of the aftercare. It is extraordinary how much two or three people can achieve in fourteen acres; at the turn of the century there were nineteen and the head gardener rarely removed his top hat and white gloves!

In 1979, I began seriously to replan the garden, having devoted the first three years mainly to the house. I started with a delightful, small walled space running east to west, intersected by flagstoned paths with squares of grass and borders about three feet wide, which had been the dumping-ground for clinker from some historic fire. The main problem was to find cohesion in an area of hot sun and deep shade. I drew up extensive plans, and fortunately at this time met the Boyd-Carpenters, sadly both now dead, who had taken over Margery Fish's famous garden at East Lambrook. They endorsed my tentative ideas and supplied many of the plants. I well remember Gordon gently telling me I had stuck a hedera cutting in upside down!

Grey, silver and variegated became the theme. Artemisias, *Stachys olympica* (*S. lanata*), caryopteris, *Phlomis fruticosa*, *Atriplex halimus*, *Ballota pseudo-dictamnus*, *Pyrus salicifolia* and pinks are some of the plants on the sunny side. Two marvellous white *Hydrangea* 'Mme E. Mouillière', which started life as pot plants in a London house, are the focal point of the shady side, grown with Japanese anemones, hostas, ferns and primulas, with *Elaeagnus pungens* 'Maculata' to brighten the darkest corner. White *Clematis montana* clothes one wall – double joy, it now tumbles over into the courtyard beyond. *Clematis orientalis* annually climbs twenty feet, covered in nodding yellow bells and silken seed heads. *Clematis* 'Marie Boisselot' thrills me each year, climbing through the atriplex and flowering a second time in October with huge, white quilted sepals. This little garden matured and looked settled within three years and needs very little maintenance. I have plans to replace the grass with flagstones and increase the low planting of things like thyme which do not mind being walked on.

The Italian Garden lent itself perfectly to the planting of herbaceous borders. My older friends all threw fits and advised me against them, because of the enormous amount of work involved, but undeterred and feeling, hopefully, I had another thirty years to change my mind, I went ahead. Each border is prefixed by an ancient *Magnolia* x *soulangiana* and divided by fifteen-foot-high, six-foot-thick yew hedges. A herringbone brick path, the ideal foil between lawn and border, echoing the back-drop of the kitchen garden wall, was discovered under the grass, which we peeled off like a roll of carpet. In my desire to fill space quickly, I established a holding ground in the kitchen garden, where I grew plants from seed and cuttings (often given by our volunteer stewards who look after the house on open days). Packets of seeds yielded thousands of plants, few of which I could bear to throw away. Since then, I have learnt to be selective and have become an avid plant collector, rarely leaving home without returning with some new treasure.

The first border, planted in the spring of 1984, is a composition of soft colours – blues, mauves, pinks and white – with a few background shrubs, notably *Buddleja fallowiana alba*, *B. alternifolia*, and *Rosa glauca* (*R. rubrifolia*) with its lovely pewter foliage and single pink blooms. The second border comes as a bit of a shock: hiding behind the buttress of yew, it has all the stronger colours, from cream through yellow, gold, bronze, orange and red. This border was planted in 1985 and is still undergoing various changes and additions. I am always amazed at the way plants behave differently in varying situations. Give them good soil, warmth and shelter, and plants of quite manageable proportions very quickly become giants.

The herringbone path leads to the woodland under tall old *Rhododendron ponticum*. This area was a dense wilderness, which we cleared to leave the lovely old trees free-standing. Sadly a lot of the good woodland soil went too; this has slowly been rectified by tipping the autumn leaves here for several seasons. I longed for wonderful hydrangeas, rhododendrons, kalmias and other exotic beauties. Unforeseen was the amount of moisture these shrubs need, as well as shade and shelter. The big trees were providing too much shade and drinking all the available moisture, so there have been various changes of site here, together with some tree surgery to remove a few low-slung branches. I am continuing to plant foxgloves, bluebells, ferns

127 The water rills flowing between conical yew trees, looking towards the south front.

128 The second herbaceous border dominated by *Achillea filipendulina* 'Gold Plate', interspersed with spires of self-seeding *Verbascum*, probably *bombyciferum*.

127

128

129

130

and other woodland plants and hope one day this area will repay the labour.

The balustraded forecourt faces east and has symmetrical borders around the base of the walls. It is interesting to see that the north-facing border is always at least two weeks later than its southern twin. These borders are planted with softly coloured Hybrid Musk roses, namely 'Pax', 'Penelope', 'Cornelia' and 'Buff Beauty'. They are not ideal perhaps, needing more space than they are allowed here, but with surreptitious pruning they are a glorious sight in June and July. I have planted climbing roses against the walls to lengthen the season and have also underplanted these borders, because I hate to see roses growing out of bare soil. *Ajuga reptans* 'Burgundy Glow' is a purple-leaved version of the wild bugle; it is smothered in short blue flowers in early summer. *Polygonum affine* 'Darjeeling Red' is a rampant plant but, confined between grass and wall, is easily controlled and of great merit. Blocking out all weeds, it flowers for weeks with elegant deep pink spikes in late summer, and its foliage turns a handsome rusty brown in winter. These two ground cover plants are interspersed with clumps of nepeta, although mine is rather large and untidy. I simply love the combination of

catmint and roses in large bowls indoors.

Four tall stone pillars punctuate this courtyard, with the rose 'Albertine' climbing up them. Like most ramblers, it is a difficult rose to train, but its incomparable colour and perfume make it worth a little effort. We have added more pillars for the full and lovely pink rose 'Constance Spry'. I am attempting to train small flowered white clematis up these wooden pillars to give the rose some support and to strengthen the picture, but so far I have only succeeded in achieving the desired effect with one out of six. Although I adore the roses, I generally find that they are difficult to maintain in perfect condition. We treat them all every month with a three-in-one spray, which is a feed, insecticide and fungicide, yet some still seem to catch every bug and disease possible. Roses beautifully trained – horizontally along walls, around pillars and in their allocated space in borders in the winter – develop an exuberance in summer which is hard to control. Only the Rugosas seem trouble-free and happy to be left alone.

Perhaps my favourite place is the herb border, which begins outside the massive oak back door, where *Hedera helix* 'Glacier' climbs elegantly round a mullioned window in fairly deep shade. I can see the

131

132

length of this border while sitting at the kitchen table and am therefore more critical of it than of other areas. The border runs along the base of a high wall, part of which is a wing of the house, and is backed by climbers. *Vitis coignetiae* is the glory of this wall; its creamy leaves with tan underneath appear in spring, gradually covering the wall until the autumn, when they turn the most glorious shades from orange to reddish-purple. Fig trees grow against the lower part and are really a pest; they should be in retaining beds to restrict them, but of course they are not and put on an enormous amount of growth each year. The figs are delicious when the frost does not do for them.

Last is the huge walled kitchen garden, only a shadow of its former glory, but nevertheless a haven of peace and shelter. One day, when we're old, I'd like a little house at the south end of this lovely space, with a tower to enable us to view the wooded valley. Until then, the excitement of watching and helping this garden develop for ourselves and the public to enjoy, will, I hope, be undiminished.

Jennie Makepeace.

129 Late summer in the herb border, with *Ruta graveolens* 'Jackman's Blue', in front of *Laurus nobilis*, with a tendril of *Vitis coignetiae* in autumn colours.

130 View across the yew-tree terraces in summer.

131 A corner of the front forecourt with wisteria and a clump of *Geranium ibericum*.

132 *Nepeta* 'Six Hills Giant' and *Polygonum affine* 'Darjeeling Red', in front of the Hybrid Musk rose 'Pax'.

Mrs Anne Dexter's garden, OXFORD, OXFORDSHIRE

It was in 1957 that I moved from a large garden to a small one – a *very* small one.

The terraced house in Victorian north Oxford opened, on its south side, on to a narrow rectangle of ground, seven yards wide by twenty-five yards long, with a five-foot high, mellow red-brick wall along either side and a wooden fence along the bottom. How could I possibly accommodate all the plants I would want to grow, I wondered. The prospect appeared distinctly limited.

After completing essential alterations to the house I was able to concentrate thought and effort on my neglected plot with its so-called 'lawn', gnarled old shrubs, worn-out perennials and large rowan tree which shaded half the area. Everything was cleared except a pink climbing rose which, I discovered, flowered on and off throughout the summer.

It was not difficult to decide against grass in favour of paving for a not quite straight, off-centre path and for a square sitting-out 'terrace' on the sunny place immediately outside the French windows. A load of thirty-eight square yards of broken paving-stones was ordered and duly delivered; the delivery man was not best pleased to find that every piece had to be carried through the house, there being no side access. The ground was levelled as best I could and, after many hours of back- and arm-aching work, the last stone was laid.

The length is divided into three, but not formally,

because of limited space; the south-facing area leading from the 'terrace' is the alpine garden, which merges into the herbaceous or mixed border, while the far third is a 'greenery' or shade garden. From this simple basic plan the garden has evolved over the years, a strong stimulus being an ever-growing desire to create space for more and more plants. One of my earliest extensions was achieved by erecting wooden panels of squared trellis three feet above the east and west boundary walls to accommodate climbers and scramblers. This erection was the only task for which I have called in outside help.

A less conventional device was the implantation of twelve-foot poles, which were sturdy sawn-off tree saplings with their side shoots shortened to six inches, set against and wired to the walls. Four of these poles on either side are linked by a thick rope wrapped around with wire-netting to make swags for clematis – mostly the small-flowered sorts like *Clematis viticella* and its hybrids, and 'Perle d'Azur' and 'Mrs George Jackman' – which clamber above the mixed border. Another ploy is the close-planting of standard *Malus* with different coloured foliage, placed three feet from the west wall, their tops pleached by regular pruning to direct their growth sideways.

All this natural and artificial treillage is required for the climbing roses and for my thirty-five selected clematis, which scramble through whatever is nearest, including the shrubs planted at the base of the walls. Frequently they are given guidance: for example *Clematis* 'Etoile Rose' may be coaxed over a *Prunus* x *cistena*, which is not there by chance. Clematis flourish here and are a tremendous asset since their flowering season is from spring until the first frosts.

133 By late summer, clematis have been drawn forward over shrubs and rose bushes to give the last splendid display of the year. *Clematis* 'Victoria' and *C. pisifera* 'Mme Julia Correvon' with *Chamaecyparis obtusa* 'Snow' and *Berberis thunbergii* 'Gold Ring'.

Shrubs are chosen for foliage, character and colour. They range from the yellows of privet, golden elm and *Robinia pseudacacia* 'Frisia' (the latter kept to a slender column) through to the purple of *Cotinus coggygria* 'Foliis Purpureis', *Berberis thunbergii* 'Somerset' and *B.* x *ottawensis*. They are close planted and consequently have to be pruned once, twice or even three times a year to keep them strictly to their allotted spaces.

The fence at the end is screened by a tapestry of foliage forms arranged in three layers, from a fifteen-foot-high *Elaeagnus* x *ebbingei* and golden elder at the back, to four-foot high plants in the front. X *Fatshedera lizei*, *Fatsia japonica* and *Aucuba japonica* 'Crotonifolia' are there, contrasting with the smaller foliage of *Cornus alba* 'Elegantissima', *Viburnum* x *burkwoodii*, the silver and golden variegated privets and others. Tall poles support *Vitis coignetiae*, *Clematis montana* 'Alexander' and a golden-leaved hop. A purple *Prunus* x *cistena* picks up the purple colours which run through both sides of the garden, as does a *Prunus cerasifera* 'Pissardii', which is the sole mature standard tree in the garden.

In the centre of the boundary fence is an oak door. Once, on a garden visit, I was deceived by a large mirror at the end of a long path. It was not fitting to try it here, but I conceived the idea of a door, with a lightly trimmed golden privet around it, which might beckon one on to pass beyond and under the tall trees into the open. But, alas, that is a neighbour's property.

The shade cast by this embankment of trees and shrubs encouraged me to establish peat and leaf-mould beds on either side of the path, now lowered to allow some steps up to the door. Semi-circular excavated bays held up by dry-stone walls make homes for trilliums, *Cornus canadensis* and other western calcifuges, ramondas, haberleas, willow gentians, cyclamen, small primulas and a collection of small ferns which are spreading apace. Small hostas like *H. tokudama* make excellent foils for the frondy ferns.

Turning back towards the house, the central area with its facing twin borders is packed with pillar roses, such as 'Aloha', 'Bloomfield Abundance', 'Elmshorn', and flowering and foliage shrubs at the back with the shorter perennials in the front. Colours are carefully chosen and put together. The only one not acceptable among the predominant pink and purple is fiery orange. I find, too, that the species or very early hybrids are more elegant than later 'improved' cultivars. The cylindrical spikes of *Phlox maculata* 'Alpha',

136

sabatius), *Convolvulus althaeoides tenuissimus* and *Sphaeralcea*, which produce a long-flowering delight of interwoven pink and blue.

I am an inveterate plant hunter and incurably acquisitive. Nothing gives me greater pleasure than seeking out and visiting nurseries. Gardeners are generous givers too, so I have built up an extensive collection of all kinds of both well-known and uncommon treasures, and I try to arrange them to please the eye. It is said that plants like growing in close community and mine certainly have to do that here.

The intensive system of growing that has evolved in this tiny patch calls for a high level of nutrition and it is necessary to feed regularly with complete compound fertilisers. Even when spraying against aphis and other pests, I add a proprietary foliar feed. Using a spray-gun attached to the garden hose I can get round the whole garden in two 'goes'.

Watering becomes essential after only a few dry days, particularly in hot or windy weather. I have to remind myself that rain does not readily penetrate the thick foliage and that clematis are the first to suffer from dryness at the roots.

If my garden is labour-intensive out of proportion to its size, I am richly rewarded. I live with an ever-changing tapestry of colour throughout the year. I can observe in close-up — indeed I am almost forced to — the incredible variety of foliage forms and textures and the exquisitely delicate designs and patterns of my large family of flowers.

which is rose-pink, and 'Omega', which is white, are examples of this.

The perennials are supported by two-inch mesh wire-netting surrounds, each supported by four canes. In autumn the netting is rolled up, firmly stamped upon and stored in the cellar.

The alpine beds are nearest the house and lead from the paved terrace where they get maximum sun. All beds have gradually been raised as much as nine inches over the years by top-dressings, but here I raised them even higher by excavating to lower the path and support the sides with dry-stone walling. This gave extra planting surfaces and varied the flatness of the long, thin garden. In the sharply drained beds jostle miniature gems of the alpine and rock-garden world — dianthus, erodiums, origanums, campanulas, dwarf grasses and tiny shrubs — a host of dwarfs too numerous to list without tedium. Some flourish in a collection of small stone troughs collected by my mother in Cumbria in the days when such things were considered rubbish on the farmsteads. Most of these containers are placed near the terrace; one larger one under the south-facing wall of the house serves to protect from frost the roots of some precious Mediterranean trailers, namely *Convolvulus mauritanicus* (now named C.

134 The sunken path increases the dry-wall area over which plants drape themselves. In the left foreground are *Campanula carpatica* and *Eryngium bourgatii*. Purple-leaved cultivars of *Berberis thunbergii* mark the beginning of the herbaceous section.

135 The middle section of this narrow garden, where herbaceous perennials jostle. Purple-leaved berberises are set off by silver *Artemisia* 'Powis Castle' and *A. ludoviciana*; blue *Clematis* x *durandii* climbs over *Lonicera nitida* 'Baggesen's Gold' while *Clematis* 'Perle d'Azur' rampages high above.

136 The *trompe l'oeil* at the end of the path — a wooden door set in a high, narrow 'hedge' of shrubs which supports climbers such as golden hop, large-leaved variegated ivy (*Hedera colchica* 'Dentata Variegata') and clematis. The lace-cap hydrangea 'Lanarth White' is on the left.

Miss Joan Loraine's garden, PORLOCK, SOMERSET

It is January 27. This morning, before recording the weather or watering the cutting frames, I placed a bottle of sherry by the back door so that there would be no delay should it be needed – there have been years when the sun has vanished while I was looking for the sherry. The sun only returns for a few minutes this first day, striking the bottom lawn at the foot of a stalwart oak, lighting the furrows in the bark and the sea-green lichen. But today, when it reached the dip in the hills through which it should have shone down on us for the first time since November, rain was falling. So no libation was poured out in thanksgiving.

The yearly retreat and return of the sun is our Advent. A clearly defined shadow moves forward in front of us, engulfing the fields below, and then the fields beyond, till only the reed bed and waters of the marsh, the shingle bank and rocky forehead of Hurlstone glint in sunlight beside the Severn Sea. Then, with the turn of the year, the line of shadow comes nearer, taking sudden leaps after a spell of grey days, until we greet the sun once more. And so, some while later, does the steep hillside behind us, the wooded tumble of Exmoor to the sea.

Greencombe is a strip of three and a half acres on the edge of ancient woodland, above Porlock's long-tilled fields. It is called after the combe behind it, the only one in this arc of hills with a sward of grass but no water. So, we are stream-less; moreover, we tip into the face of the dominant north-west wind. We have a long stretch of fencing to maintain (and to conceal, so as to appear without limits), six feet high to keep out red deer. The site is steep; there is no soil, only stone

137 Deciduous azaleas in flower, with apple trees above and the fields of Porlock Marsh below.

and the leaf-mould of centuries; and light intensity is low.

I never visit other gardens without thinking how much easier they must be than Greencombe – easier for plants, let alone gardeners. But I return to rejoice in the unexpected riches of this place.

Today the golden petals of witch hazel glisten against the purple-brown of winter oak, and winter sweet hangs pale beside a twenty-foot columnar Lawson cypress; both shrubs were out for Christmas and provided festive fragrance throughout the house. (I have learnt to select a large branch for cutting, not to nibble, as neither grows gracefully afterwards.) *Rhododendron dauricum*, blooming for the first time, is a song of bright purple. *Camellia sasanqua*, with its wild rose flowers, crimson and white varieties intertwined, is brilliant along the vegetable garden wall. *Crocus imperati* is up, lovely and scented, but one of my mistakes, for its cups remain closed without sun.

Best of all, five weeks early, *Rhododendron giganteum* (now, alas, called *R. protistum* var. *giganteum*) is coming into magnificent bloom, with wide trusses of bright rose-magenta bells astride the foot-long, deeply veined leaves – leaves of such substance that even two years after they have fallen they lie in decorative litter, still entire. Only the new growth looks tender when it bursts through brilliant red bracts, held upright, like candles, in May.

It was the dramatic beauty of this young growth, and the quality of the leaves, that alerted me to the value of the plant, for I inherited this garden and did not know what was here. My first long summer, twenty years ago, was spent looking, absorbing the personalities of plants and the combination of shapes.

The garden proper, the acre round the house, was then twenty years old. It leads west into First Wood, which was then fifteen, while Far Wood, further west again, was only eight. These are the years under cultivation, not the ages of individual plants. The original oaks, sweet chestnuts and hollies are considerably older, while much has been transplanted and hundreds of plants brought in. In the last twenty years, the garden and woods have been remade, yet they are essentially the same.

In 1932 Greencombe was a rectangle of land. Then a track through was made, skirting north and east boundaries. Next a vegetable garden was enclosed with local stone at the top of the slope. The only possible site for the house was west of the track, but near it, below the wall. So, by good luck, most of the ground lay westwards, undisturbed.

Nothing was done until 1946, when Horace Stroud, who lived here before me, levelled the slope on the west side of the house, making terraces above and below and creating a green centre the shape of a grand piano. It was well done; governed by the width of the house and the position of septic tank and drains below and wall above, he made the heart of the garden beautifully. From here, you can climb stone steps which lead under an archway, also his, and through the wall; you can overlook the lower lawn, without seeing it completely; or you can walk westwards across the grass and explore.

Beyond the narrowest part of lawn, the garden opens out again: above, steps and a pathway rise through 'the combe', an effective grouping of rhododendrons and azaleas between the west wall and the garden edge; below, the lawn slopes between raised beds to the lower lawn; and straight ahead, leading into First Wood, lies the path – not the only one, but the main and only level one – which carries on through Far Wood to the end.

Here, where the wood is narrow, the path turns and comes back along the bottom. Below is a steep bank above a hollow, supported by a wall on the field side. This is the 'gut', a medieval device for keeping deer in (the ditch or hollow made it difficult for them to leap out), which dates from the thirteenth-century deer park.

The path leads back, past other paths which you can follow, and brings you to the lower lawn, a curve between the lower terrace, now above you, and the long bed below. You come out above the bottom lawn – and the view over fields to the sea.

I was no gardener when I started here. What I know, Greencombe itself has taught me, more than the many books I have read, although these too were valuable. In the identification of plants I was helped by Wisley, and this was made a delight by my near neighbour, Norman Hadden, who gave freely from his great knowledge, and from whose fabled garden at Underway I received countless cuttings and seeds. My first gardener also taught me a great deal. He had lived close to the earth all his life and was adept in the use of tools, a man of strength and of shrewd sense.

Those days were golden. But there was trouble in Paradise. Even during the first summer, I had to peg layers and take cuttings. We were losing plants which, when dug up and examined, were found to have practically no roots, only the tell-tale bootlaces of honey fungus.

This killer had been encouraged by edging paths with birch trunks and using oak and chestnut to form planting ledges. It took five years to clear the timber.

There is no space to indicate further adventures. We have only begun. I recall with joy my mother's interest and our discoveries together, and salute thankfully my marvellous workers – Ernest Barrow, Alec James, Adrian Morris, our tree surgeon – and those who are still with me, Jon Grant and Paul Keal who, between them, put in six days a week. Without them, nothing would have been possible. Surely, behind every English woman's garden, there must be a sound and willing English man.

Joan Loraine

138 The fragrant *Rhododendron* 'Lady Alice Fitzwilliam', splashed with sunshine, beside the columnar Lawson cypress at the beginning of First Wood. *Rhododendron tephropeplum* is coming into bloom on the right, and *Choisya ternata* is performing under *Camellia japonica* 'Charles Cobb' by the gateway on to the lawn.

139 *Erythronium tuolumnense* and *E. revolutum* 'White Beauty' growing with native wood sorrel in Far Wood.

140 *Rhododendron protistum* var. *giganteum*, with its candles of red leaf bracts, and *Thujopsis dolabrata* in the background.

141 *Arisaema consanguineum*: the long tails on the pitchers lead insects to the flowers; the long tails on the leaves shed water. Behind, the white flowers of *Deutzia scabra*.

138

139

140

141

The Lady FitzWalter's garden, GOODNESTONE, KENT

I think if you asked anyone who had visited Goodnestone regularly which part of the garden they preferred, without exception their answer would be 'the walled garden'. This area, almost unchanged structurally for well over 200 years, with its long central vista, between pairs of brick piers, to the tower of the village church, possibly does fulfil many people's ideal of an old-fashioned English garden. An equally old, double avenue of horse chestnuts, which flanks the now disused carriage drive and has been adopted by a colony of rooks, runs parallel outside the western wall, providing invaluable extra shelter. Immediately outside this wall is the smaller, newly restored holly avenue along which Jane Austen 'went to church down the holly walk'. Beyond the eastern wall can be seen the seventeenth-century dower house, its tiled roof worthy of Hans Andersen. The enclosed area in between seems to bask in an air of peacefulness reminiscent of another age.

The garden falls naturally into three distinct parts: the formally terraced lawns, designed in the 1840s and divided centrally by elegant flights of steps, lead in one direction to the woodland area designed and planted in the 1920s by my husband's aunt, Emily FitzWalter, and this in turn leads back into the walled garden.

We came to the house in 1955, by which time the whole place had been neglected for twenty years and the house unoccupied by the family for nearly as long. It had been requisitioned by the army during the war, towards the end of which a prisoner-of-war camp was set up, with Nissen huts built in and around the garden. Having been trained as a pianist, the idea of ruining my hands was initially rather abhorrent to me. Yet everywhere was overgrown, with just the tops of cedars and other treasures peeping out. The walled garden was derelict, except for some trailing wire and very sad espalier trees, with two great gashes in the walls where trees had blown down. It was a daunting sight; but somehow everywhere was this air of peace and tranquillity, as though the garden was quite happy and not fussed at being neglected.

Our first job was to tidy the area immediately around the house. In 1959 we took on John Wellard, a sixteen-year-old from the next-door village who wanted to garden. Thirty years later he is still with us and has become a skilled and knowledgeable gardener. That first winter he broke up the concrete bases of the Nissen huts and I sent off to Kew various plants for identification. We grassed the long gravel paths to save labour, grubbed out tree roots and cleared away brambles and nettles. I visited Sissinghurst and immediately saw the roses there fitting into Goodnestone. We went to RHS shows and were advised to buy this and that, and I scoured catalogues and read descriptions of plants – especially roses. We experimented endlessly, with some good results and as many disastrous ones. John became a skilful propagator, so we would buy one of something and increase it – but oh, so slowly. The garden – about fifteen acres in all – was so large, and we never seemed to make any impression on it. But all the time I was putting in a few roses every year – 'Nevada' and 'Maigold' in huge clumps on the long, open lower terrace in front of the house, and 'Fantin Latour', 'Koenigin von Danemark',

142 The famous view in the walled garden, with the church as its main feature. Rose 'Mme Alfred Carrière' covers the end wall, with a century-old wisteria and clematis growing on tripods.

143

144

'Tuscany' and many others in a border running away from one side of the house.

Looking back now, I am glad that our restoration and replanting took so long – it is still continuing – for we have hardly ruffled the sense of establishment from the years before. The peaceful atmosphere is still there. I almost mind more about that than I do about the plants – and the plants do flourish.

The front terraces now have a number of beds filled largely with shrubs: viburnums, species syringa, daphnes, philadelphus (including the tiny *microphyllus* with the real orange scent), with large groups of regale lilies and potentillas for late summer colouring. The winter of 1984–5 took its toll and we lost a twenty-year-old *Pittosporum tenuifolium*, which has left a large gap. The fluorescent Rugosa rose 'Blanc Double de Coubert', planted with some of the philadelphus, is a good combination, and somehow reduces a large area at one end of the bottom terrace, where the climbing rose 'Wedding Day' (planted the year John Wellard and his wife Pat were married) pours out of a very large and old juniper. On the top terrace all the planting seems dwarfed by a venerable sweet chestnut, probably put in, along with others close by in the park, when the house was built in 1704.

While the area around the house was starting to grow, we were busy in the walled garden. More roses – 'Constance Spry' with 'Cardinal de Richelieu', 'Complicata', 'Tuscany Superb', 'Buff Beauty', 'Chapeau de Napoléon' and many others – were underplanted with pinks and grey foliage plants, until the pinks got tired of our soil and refused to flourish. Now we have hardy geraniums, *Veronica incana*, with its bright blue spikes, Hidcote lavender and, in between the roses, for added height, clematis smothering tall wooden tripods – mainly *C. macropetala* and *C.m.* 'Markham's Pink' for early colouring, followed by 'Etoile Violette' and several of the *viticella* hybrids, which are accommodating and never grow too big.

As the walled garden is divided into four distinct areas, we try to have a theme which carries on from one to the next. There are roses throughout, but with other variations: a large bed of hemerocallis with small potentillas, yellow marjoram, R. 'Thisbe', *Digitalis lutea* and *D. grandiflora* (*D. ambigua*). Another border is blue with delphiniums, and *Salvia farinacea* and *S. uliginosa* to take over when the delphiniums are finished; also ceratostigma and *Salvia patens*, moving on to santolinas and the marvellous red of *Lobelia cardinalis* and *Rosa glauca* (*R. rubrifolia*). On the far

end wall beneath the church tower is a wisteria which must be decades old and part of Emily FitzWalter's original planting. After several failures and now that, at last, we are getting rid of the couch grass, agapanthus is flourishing along its base.

The walls are so beautiful with their mellow old red brick that we are loath to cover them completely and are forever changing the plants that grow up them – controlling the over-vigorous clematis and roses and adding some gentler and tenderer plants such as a young *Carpenteria californica* and *Fremontodendron californicum*. A free-standing *Magnolia grandiflora* of unusual size also somehow withstands our bitter East Kent winds, producing its luxuriant flowers, smelling of lemon nectar, from late summer right through until the end of autumn. Another of my scented, flowering favourites is the very old and large *Abelia triflora*, which drapes itself over the peculiar flint-arched gate into the walled garden and on a late summer evening is second to none. The walled garden is somewhere to wander, with the cawing of the rooks and the church tower making it all the more special.

The woodland area is quite different – a place where we can experiment with peat-loving plants in a small outcrop of acid soil, but all the time we are battling against brambles, bracken and nettles, as this was the last part to be rediscovered, and bore the brunt of the POW camp. Several of Emily FitzWalter's original plantings have survived: a *Nothofagus fusca*, *Magnolia hypoleuca* (*obovata*), the sweet-smelling balsam poplar and philadelphus, which now tower over one's head. Most of the ground is very moist, and as a result everything puts on spectacular growth. *Magnolia wilsonii*, with its hanging flowers, I love, and we have also added many of the x *soulangiana* group, eucryphias, various cornus, *Stewartia malacodendron* and *S. pseudocamellia*, which all grow away in this rare piece of non-chalk. An umbrella pine sadly succumbed but makes a good host for *Clematis montana* and the rambling rose 'Sanders' White Rambler'.

So I could go on. With our five sons grown up, I now

143 A small pond in the woodland garden.

144 Rose 'Henri Martin' under-planted with the *Penstemon* 'Heavenly Blue'.

145 The main rose garden with R. 'Complicata', 'Constance Spry', 'Gypsy Boy' and others, planted with rue, hardy geraniums, pinks and other grey-leaved plants.

133

146

have more time to read books on gardening and planning gardens, and the more I read the more I realise how little I know. I am afraid that I still tend to buy a shrub or plant because I like it, or its smell, rather than because it is the right plant for the right place. I know this is quite wrong, but I cannot resist it. On numerous occasions my long-suffering husband has waited in the car while I visit a nursery and has then had to fit everything in when I come out laden. He tends to get landed with all the jobs nobody else wants to do – but he insists that he enjoys edging. Certainly the garden has always been the more enjoyable because it has been a partnership. He has a great love (and considerable knowledge) of trees; being a purist he prefers pure foliage specimens to flowering ones. In 1984 we planted a new avenue of limes, along what was a vista shown on an original eighteenth-century plan of the park, to mark three rather special family events. Throughout all the years we have been immensely encouraged by Tom Wright of Wye College – his enthusiasm has helped more than I can say.

To me a garden is like a piece of music; each person brings his or her own interpretation to it. The people who come to see the garden are our audience and I would not be without them. Their enjoyment and pleasure – and their criticisms – make it all so worthwhile. I hope also that I have passed on to at least one of my sons my love of gardens and gardening.

146 Rose 'Fritz Nobis' in full flower, with 'Munstead' lavender and crinums.

147 A glimpse of the house framed by *Rosa glauca* and Rose 'Felicité Parmentier'.

148 A peaceful view of the woodland with *Salix fargesii*, deutzias, and *Clematis montana* growing through the rhododendrons.

Margaret FitzWalte

147

148

Mrs Sarah Bott's garden, STEVENAGE, HERTFORDSHIRE

We inherited this property, on its ancient hilltop site 300 feet above sea level, in 1970. We were full of enthusiasm and luckily ignorant of the headaches it would give us, or we would probably have turned the cows out into the garden straightaway.

The Saxons and Normans, realising the potential of the site overlooking the Beane valley, had built a palace, castle and church. The old defences are still intact and even now it would be difficult for robbers to get away easily. The flint keep is ruined but the church remains to stand guardian on the other side of the moat. At the beginning of the eighteenth century a wonderful folly appeared when James Pulham, an innovator from Woodbridge, built a magnificent 'Norman' gatehouse, curtain wall and summer house linking the ruins to the house. The summer house has a buddha in a niche above a marble tablet from the Field of Troy commemorating a Greek slave. It really is a folly. In 1906 my husband's grandparents came home from India and bought the estate. They were responsible for a large addition to the house and a verandah, and for the garden.

Our place in the cycle has been to restore the garden. It was sleeping peacefully in the hands of my in-laws and Jim and Edith Collis, who had worked in it for fifty years but were due to retire. Before the war there had been five gardeners but, by 1970, with Jim and Edith alone and part-time, a few new ideas were needed. The bones and roots were all there, which was lucky as I know I could not make a garden from a ploughed field.

149 Gold and silver beds in the kitchen garden, planted by Ian to replace bedding schemes from Edwardian days.

First we bought a goat to clear out the overgrown moat – a fine idea as long as he did not escape to prune anything else. My husband remembered the days when the big lawn had been mown, so we bought a large Hayter and told our weekend visitors to get busy and sweat off the London gin. We also obtained a knapsack sprayer to tackle the bindweed and brambles. But inevitably there were disasters. By the time nineteen elms as big as dinosaurs had been removed and the great drought of 1976 had run its course, the place looked like a desert. I remember my total despair as I struggled to keep our first new plants alive with water from the washing-up bowl.

Jim retired completely after that summer and Ian Billot arrived from Scotland. He is a tremendous enthusiast and a very skilled propagator, so we decided to open the grounds and sell plants to help with the finances. Ten years later it is nearly all in apple pie order and we are able to enjoy the garden with the visitors, some of whom return again and again to note the latest improvement and have become very good friends.

The original layout is more or less intact except that nearly all the beds are smaller. The overgrown shrubberies have been cleared and replanted and the endless steep grass banks tamed with a strimmer. This one machine has probably done more to help the garden than any other. Ian is responsible for two new features: a woodland walk round the outer bailey and another walk round the back of the pond.

I am nothing but a copycat and my ideas all come from visiting other gardens. Hatfield House is just down the road and always an inspiration. I think the two books I owe most to are Russell Page's *Education*

of a Gardener and Vita Sackville-West's *Garden Book* – the first for the maxim of restraint, so important with trees and shrubs, the second for the enthusiasm it imparts to a beginner. More recently, Jane Brown's *Gardens of a Golden Afternoon* has enthralled me.

This is a garden of the golden afternoon. The grass tennis court is in full view of the verandah and the cucumber sandwiches, and behind it the big lawn stretches away down the hill to magnificent open country separated from the park by the big pond. In true Edwardian tradition, there are several well-kept secrets tucked away from this spectacular view. A wide terrace below the verandah leads left-handed to the moat and right-handed to a sunken garden surrounded by yew hedges with a lead statue of Shylock in the centre. He stands among old English lavender and a succession of summer flowers. It is a sheltered and peaceful spot, which leads into the rockery.

The rockery is my particular department. It has three little pools fed by a spring and small beds slope in towards the pools. There are not many alpine plants now, but it is full of small shrubs, plants with interesting leaves and spring bulbs. Every autumn a thick layer of peat is put on the beds, which makes weeding very easy. Inevitably I am always behind with the weeding,

so primulas, violets, bluebells, hellebores, primroses, corydalis and foxgloves seed themselves everywhere. I like it that way.

Behind the rockery, next to the kitchen garden and running down the hill from top to bottom, are the double herbaceous borders. A backing of the lilac and rose 'Canary Bird' starts them off in the spring, and then through the summer, like great men, they 'strive ever upwards through the night' and are an unsophisticated jungle of iris, poppies, roses, lupins, delphiniums, hollyhocks and many more old favourites. Like the rockery, the beds are kept heavily mulched to try and prevent the dreadful cracks which appear by August in the solid clay soil.

A path leads between the borders and through an iron gate into the kitchen garden across to the greenhouse and plant centre. In the past the narrow beds on each side of the grass path were full of bedding plants, but Ian has planted mixed gold and silver borders and the few remaining fruit trees have roses climbing over them. Gradually, as our need for vegetables gets less, flowers are appearing in the kitchen garden. There is a herb garden, and I am planning an autumn border with lots of Michaelmas daisies and penstemons. It is in the kitchen garden that the more unusual Beth

Chatto sort of plants are grown, propagated and sold.

Back at the house, I must mention the courtyard, which is enclosed by the folly and house walls. This is the most sheltered place in the garden and here we foolishly try to grow things that are not totally hardy. Inevitably they come and go, but we have succeeded with some, including a fremontodendron. There is a very large white *Magnolia* x *soulangiana* surviving from the grandparents' day, which was bought in Hertford Market for 7s. 6d.

In front of the house there is a formal rose garden which has been completely replanted in the last five years. The roses have all been chosen for their scent and are mostly 'Margaret Merril' and 'Radox Bouquet', two roses bred by Harkness of Hitchin. Thymes, lavenders and pinks are being planted with them, so

150 South-west view from the house across the lawn to the park. White iris and rosemary flank the steps down to the old entrance drive.

151 Snowdrops rioting in the moat.

152 Top half of the herbaceous borders in late May. Rose 'Canary Bird' providing early colour with pyrethrums and lupins.

152

153

154

we are hoping to have a scented froth of pink, white and grey.

Finally, my great loves are the winter-flowering plants. I want a garden all the year, not just in the summer, so the original winter garden which was confined to the keep has spread all round the ruin. Several attempts have at last established *Hamamelis mollis* and I am proud of the row of *Prunus subhirtella* 'Autumnalis' which can be seen from the house behind the roses. The snowdrops rioting over the moat and around the ruins are famous now and are spreading all over the garden. They are followed by sheets of scillas and daffodils. I am slowly establishing the gentle wild daffys from Cornwall, which are so much more attractive than the modern hybrids.

I think that to walk round in the dusk in the winter, with the pheasants going to bed, and to be able to pick a posy of flowers makes one sure that a garden is worthwhile. How lucky we are to have this one, with its atmosphere and history.

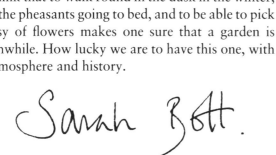

153 Looking north along the path which separates the orchard from the kitchen garden. Rose 'Nevada', philadelphus and Rose 'Flora McIver' climbing up *Prunus* 'Ukon'.

154 Shylock demanding his pound of flesh amid a bower of *Clematis* 'Nelly Moser' and white iris. Rose 'Iceberg' and *Lilium auratum* flower later, their white flowers marrying well with the lead statue.

155 Rock garden, looking south, in May with the top pond and the park in the background. Pink lily tulips complement campion and a variety of euphorbias and Spring greens.

156 The herbaceous borders, a major feature, from the bottom of the garden. Rose 'Fritz Nobis' in the foreground.

155

156

Mrs M. St J. V. Gibbs' garden,
CIRENCESTER, GLOUCESTERSHIRE

About 150 years ago, this house was moved half a mile from the other side of the River Thames. The garden was made five hundred yards from the house, inside a beautiful Cotswold stone wall. We like to think that the lovely old cedar trees, very tall limes and the rows of elm trees down the drive and around the orchard were planted at that time.

When we came here in 1947, there was no garden as such, only large areas of lawn – or rather grass fields – with overgrown yew hedges and mature but totally dead cedars very close to the house. Now I really regret not having planted an exciting ornamental tree for summer shade in their place when we felled them.

Making a garden of all this was a real challenge. The area was roughly divided into four: a pond full of rubble, surrounded by lawn and yew hedge; a long empty border with a high yew hedge behind and a row of round golden yews in front; and an area of lawn, large enough for croquet, with a fascinating round summerhouse at the end. On the other side of the house was a large grass area, a wartime potato patch, backed by yew trees, and a very large cedar. Another field had obviously been planted as an orchard of apples and pears, which seldom bore any fruit on such stony soil. The areas of grass and stone walls and yew hedges were there, so our ideas were dictated by these outlines. We cut the grass endlessly to make lawns, trimmed several feet off the yew hedges and eventually, with two German prisoners-of-war to help weed and dig, we were able to start planning and planting shrubs and a herbaceous border.

157 Early spring in the walled garden, the sycamore just in leaf in the background, with the old cedar in front.

A local dry-stone waller made walls and steps in the rough potato patch, dividing it into a rose garden. This was my husband's personal garden. Eleven beds, each planted with different Hybrid Tea roses, were a wonderful sight in June, a blaze of colour – dark red, apricot, pink and yellow – and a wonderful scent when all in flower. Sadly, twelve years later, the roses started dying back and the labour involved in pruning, spraying and deadheading five hundred roses became too time-consuming. We had to replan and made the area into four corner beds and a central paved area. Two original roses were incorporated into two of the corner beds: 'Queen Elizabeth' must be all of twenty years old and flowers profusely, while a beautifully scented rose, 'Texas Centennial', grows happily beneath a large cedar and never fails to produce a mass of lovely deep pink flowers. The third corner bed is ablaze with alstroemeria of every colour, surrounded by three 'Frau Dagmar Hartopp' roses and a sea of low cranesbill geraniums – pink, white and blue – agapanthus, *Salvia patens*, hostas and *Sedum spectabile* to encourage the butterflies. Low shrubs and spring bulbs fill the fourth bed, while honeysuckles and *Hedera canariensis* spill over the low walls. The central paved garden, with a lovely triple stone bird bath, has become a total jungle: pink jasmine has run wild among Rose 'François Juranville'; *Euphorbia myrsinites*, a lovely, almost jade-green colour in summer, seeds into every crevice; and two large clumps of *Crinum x powellii* 'Album' and agapanthus mix with southernwood and *Daphne odora*.

My previous gardening had been in Scotland, so Cotswold brash and lime and clay were unknown to

me. What a contrast! Few of my old favourites would grow and I made many mistakes in trying to coax them into tolerating lime. It saddens me to see plants going backwards and I hate discarding them to the bonfire or compost heap. Sadly I am unable to grow my special favourites from childhood, massed primulas, in this soil. As a child of ten or eleven I was lucky enough to be given a tiny greenhouse by my father, who was a very good gardener, and I spent hours growing seeds and taking cuttings, so I have always loved propagating and have increased roses and shrubs as well as perennial plants for many years in our garden here.

For about ten years, with a growing family, I had little time to do much active work and only kept the garden tidy, but, with help, we made a vegetable and fruit garden in part of an orchard field. Again – endless stones and lime and clay predominating – it took very hard work to make a reasonable tilth, but eventually, after countless loads of manure, leaf mould and compost, we were ready and at last had a vegetable garden. For the last six years we have been very fortunate in having Peter Measures, an energetic and hardworking young gardener, who has worked diligently and helped me keep everything in good order.

It wasn't easy to obtain plants at the end of the war, as everyone's garden had been cultivated for food. 'Dig for Victory' being the slogan, herbaceous plants were hard to come by. However, various kind friends and relations gave us loads of uninteresting clumps of divided plants, which filled an otherwise totally empty space. Garden centres did not exist, but I bought delphiniums, peonies and lupins when firms started selling again. Sadly I never ordered enough plants, but they soon increased and are still flowering happily each summer. I have, over the years, planted *Lilium candidum* and *L. regale*, *Crambe cordifolia*, shrub roses, potentillas, cistus, euphorbias and, latterly, more shrubs in order to eliminate bedding out. Shrub roses grow well on the bank by the tennis court, along with a lovely *Magnolia* x *soulangiana*, which has managed to survive some bad winters. We planted a lot of shrubs, but wish we had planted more. *Cornus nuttallii* has been a bonus; although it doesn't like lime and is not very large, it gives great joy in the summer. We found a carpet of aconites, daffodils and spring bulbs under the elms on the drive and also in the wild garden, and have increased them with more planting.

As the years went on, we had to make the big decision to fell all the elms along the drive. They were very tall and made a long green tunnel as they met

159

160

overhead in summer, but as winter storms took their toll the gaps grew wider and wider. We replaced them with alternate purple and green Norway maples and they are now sizeable trees. They make a good show in the spring, when the flowers and young buds are such a beautiful colour, and again in the autumn with a wonderful range of shades.

On the walls in front of the house there were two magnificent *Magnolia grandiflora*, which went quite forty feet up to the roof and were covered in flowers in July and August, and an old yellow Banksian rose. Sadly these all died within a few years, supposedly because the wartime service inhabitants of the house had used so much weedkiller on the gravel. It undoubtedly killed the cedars and, in time, reached these lovely magnolias. I then planted a new magnolia, which had almost reached twenty feet when it was cruelly struck down by frost and snow in 1979. Happily it is now coming again from the roots. Considering the original magnolias survived a hundred years or more, have the seasons changed, are the winters really colder? Three times our south wall has been badly hit by arctic conditions: ceanothus, actinidia, cotoneasters all killed, wisteria battered and leafless but recovered this year. A very old ilex caught

158 The round summer-house from the top lawn, with *Buddleja alternifolia* and *Cotinus coggygria* and mixed shrub roses.

159 Waterlilies in flower in the pool, with mixed alpines among the paving and *Alchemilla mollis* all around.

160 *Fremontodendron californicum* covered in bright yellow flowers, on the south front of the manor alongside a wisteria.

161

the full force of one storm and has taken a long time to look happy again. To take the eye from its nakedness, I have underplanted it with a good many hydrangeas, *Rubus* Tridel, bupleurum and a group of roses from cuttings. *Fremontodendron californicum* has reached fifteen feet after three years. The yellow flowers last from May to November, but I find it an annoying, untidy shrub, with dead flowers which will not drop off and a pile of withered flowers at its feet. Along with *Hydrangea petiolaris* it fills a large gap on the south wall.

An ancient pear tree grows on an east and south wall and has glorious blossom and, most years, lots of rather small, delicious fruit.

The other part of the garden with the lily pond is an area of lawn surrounded by a low yew hedge and paving. The pond was duly relined and filled with water; surprisingly the fountain was still in working order. The water lilies we planted flower profusely, have increased tremendously and have to be thinned out at times. The paving is rather over-full of thyme, helianthemum, a few creeping alpines and colourful alpine phlox. Round it I planted *Alchemilla mollis* to soften the outlines. The low wall and steps down to the pond garden have the original aubrieta growing over the walls.

We turned some old stables into a large garden room overlooking the lily pond. The paved area in front is a marvellous place for pots: pots of lilies, pots of petunias and geraniums, and a large pot with myrtle and a bright blue Corsican rosemary. Himalayan Musk rose ramps on the wall along with some very productive vines.

I do not think I have been influenced by any particular garden although I enjoy visiting gardens in this country and abroad.

Mary M Gibbs

161 Looking towards the wild garden from the sundial, shrub roses 'Penelope', 'Felicia', 'Camaieux', 'Fantin Latour' and 'Kazanlik' with lilies and the dense, dark leaves of a viola beneath.

Index of plants

Page numbers in italics refer to illustrations.

Abelia triflora, 133
abeliophyllum, 114
Abies cephalonica, 48, 49; *A. grandis*, 109
Abutilon, 44; *A.* x *suntense*, 37, 56, 83; *A.* x
  s. 'Jermyns', 97; *A. vitifolium*, 73; *A. v.*
  album, 98; *A. v.* 'Veronica Tennant', 97
Acacia, 96; *A. pravissima*, 115
Acaena 'Blue Haze', 109
acanthus, 71
Acer, 37, 54, 64, 99; *A. capillipes*, 76; *A.*
  circinatum, 76; *A. davidii*, 36, 59, 112,
  114; *A. ginnala*, 76, 94; *A. griseum*, 36, 45,
  114, 115; *A. grosseri hersii*, 59; *A.*
  japonicum 'Aureum', 114; *A. negundo*
  'Flamingo', 36; *A. n.* 'Variegatum', 92; *A.*
  palmatum 'Atropurpureum', 23, 57, 99; *A.*
  f. 'Sango Kaku' ('Senkaki'), 76, 114; *A.*
  platanoides 'Drummondii', 60; *A.*
  pseudoplatanus 'Brilliantissimum', 36, 37,
  45, 97; *A.* x 'Worleei', 76, 77; snake bark a.,
  44, 45, 73, 114
Achillea, 32, 102, 105; *A. filipendulina* 'Gold
  Plate', 119
Acidanthera murielae, see *Gladiolus*
  callianthus
aconite, winter, 20, 32, 46, 47, 60, 73, 101,
  144
Actinidia, 145; *A. chinensis*, 60; *A.*
  kolomikta, 75, 84
Aesculus indica, 73; *A. parviflora*, 60
Agapanthus, 36, 37, 43, 50, 98, 115, 133,
  143; *A. campanulatus*, 96
Ajuga, 114; *A.* 'Burgundy Glow', 107, 120;
  A. 'Rainbow', 107
Akebia quinata, 117
Alchemilla mollis, 20, 29, 36, 145, 146
Allium, 107, 109; *A. cernuum*, 109; *A.*
  christophii (*albopilosum*), 83, 85, 105,
  109; *A. giganteum*, 83; *A. karataviense*,
  74; *A. pulchellum*, 109; *A.*
  rosenbachianum, 83; *A. schubertii*, 94
Alnus glutinosa, 103
Alstroemeria, 36, 37, 143; *A. ligtu* hybrids,
  44, 107
Amelanchier, 19; *A. laevis*, 83
Amsonia salicifolia, 66
Anaphalis, 103; *A. margaritacea*, 71
Anchusa 'Dropmore', 49
Anemone, 58; *A. blanda*, 20, 108; *A. b.*
  'Atrocaerulea', 87; Japanese a., 32, 102,
  107, 108, 114; *A.* 'Queen Charlotte', 108;
  A. 'White Queen', 108
angelica, 100
antirrhinum, 25, 49
apple, 11, 12, 49, 59, 61, 67, 88, 88, 95, 111,

126; espalier a., 11, 13, 26; *A.* 'Nonsuch',
  50
apricot, 49, 113
Aralia elata, 58
Araucaria araucana, 109
arbutus, 114
arctotis, 114
Arisaema candidissimum, 108; *A.*
  consanguineum, 129
Arisarum proboscideum, 108
Artemisia, 25, 51, 60, 105; *A. arborescens*,
  71, 72; *A. ludoviciana*, 124; *A.* 'Powis
  Castle', 124
artichoke, 13, 26
arum, 115
Aruncus dioicus, 107
arundinaria, 114
ash, 19, 108; weeping a., 36
asparagus, 26
Aster acris, 107, 108; *A.* 'Carnival', 107; *A.* x
  frikartii, 50, 105
astilbe, 21, 22, 64, 68, 108
astrantia, 55, 100
aubrieta, 49, 87, 146
Aucuba japonica 'Crotonifolia', 124
Azalea, 44, 45, 54, 55, 56, 106, 108, 126,
  128; *A.* 'Eddy', 52; *A. pontica*, 50

Ballota pseudodictamnus, 73
bamboo, 57
barley, wild, 16, 17
bean, scarlet runner, 17
beech, 44, 78; copper b., 19, 76; golden b.,
  77; b. hedge, 45, 71, 109; purple Dawyck
  b., 77
beetroot 'Detroit', 108
Berberis x *ottawensis*, 124; purple b., 112,
  124; *B. thunbergii* 'Gold Ring', 122; *B. t.*
  'Somerset', 124
Bergenia, 32, 36, 98; *B. cordifolia*, 23
Betula (birch), 13, 19; silver b., 20, 43, 112;
  B. utilis jacquemontii, 36, 50, 97
blackberry, 16
bluebell, 22, 50, 64, 73, 78, 118, 138
bog bean, 109
bottle-brush, 97
box, 26, 43, 47, 59, 81, 82, 83, 84, 85; b.
  hedge, 76, 101, 105
broom, 17, 32
brunnera, 13
Buddleja, 14, 73; *B. alternifolia*, 118, 144; *B.*
  auriculata, 93; *B. davidii*, 17; *B. fallowiana*
  alba, 118
bulrush, 114
bupleurum, 146

buttercup, 17
buxus, 11, 20

cabbage, 108
calamintha, 33
callistemon, 115
Caltha palustris, 106
camassia, 107, 108
Camellia, 54, 55, 56, 64, 97, 108; *C. japonica*
  'Charles Cobb', 129; *C. sasanqua*, 127
Campanula, 32, 44, 82, 84, 125; *C.*
  alliariifolia 'Ivory Bells', 59; *C. burghaltii*,
  59; *C. carpatica*, 124; *C. lactiflora*, 41, 55;
  C. l. 'Loddon Anna', 94
campion, 141
Campsis, 42; *C. grandiflora*, 98
candytuft, 25, 107
Cardiocrinum giganteum, 56, 109
carnation, 79
Carpenteria californica, 56, 98, 133
Carpinus betulus, 102; *C. b.* 'Fastigiata', 97
Cassia corymbosa, 114
Castanea sativa 'Albo-marginata', 97
Catalpa, 59, 99; *C. bignonioides* 'Aurea', 76
catmint, 61, 120
Ceanothus, 83, 93, 145; *C. impressus* 'Puget
  Blue', 105; *C.* 'Topaz', 98; *C.* 'Trewithen
  Blue', 56
Cedrus (cedar), 9, 59, 71, 75, 82, 142, 145;
  C. atlantica glauca, 19, 107; *C. deodara*,
  19, 35, 99; *C. libani* (c. of Lebanon), 12,
  72, 79, 81, 111
ceratostigma, 132
Cercidiphyllum japonicum, 26, 58
chaenomeles, 98
Chamaecyparis lawsoniana, 31; *C. l.*
  'Allumii', 70; *C. l.* 'Ellwoodii' 19, 20;
  C. pisifera 'Snow', 122
cherry, 17, 50, 73, 103, 112; Japanese c., 32;
  wild c., 44
chestnut, horse, 112, 131
chestnut, sweet, 75, 111, 128, 132
Chimonanthus praecox, 79
Chionanthus virginicus, 77
chionodoxa, 15, 83, 108
chives, giant, 110
Choisya ternata, 129
Christmas rose, 50
Chrysanthemum frutescens, 30
cimicifuga, 49
Cistus, 33, 36, 37, 40, 83, 144; *C.* x
  corbariensis, 98; *C. laurifolius*, 98
Clematis, 15, 17, 26, 32, 36, 43, 44, 77, 83,
  84, 88, 89, 98, 98, 112, 114, 115, 120,
  123, 125, 125, 130, 132, 133; *C. armandii*,

Clematis Cont.

114; C. 'Barbara Dibley', 33; C. *cirrhosa balearica*, 84; C. 'Comtesse de Bouchaud', 115; C. 'Duchess of Edinburgh', 77; C. x *durandii*, 124; C. 'Etoile Rose', 123; C. 'Etoile Violette', 132; C. *flammula*, 73; C. 'Frances Rivis', 84; C. 'Huldine', 114; C. 'Jackmanii Superba', 98; C. 'Lasurstern', 86; C. *macropetala*, 132; C. *m.* 'Markham's Pink', 132; C. 'Mme Julia Correvon', 122; C. 'Marie Boisselot', 32; C. 'Miss Bateman', 84; C. 'Mrs George Jackman', 123; C. *montana*, 45, 133, 135; C. *m.* 'Alexander', 124; C. *m.* 'Rubens', 49, 110; C. 'Nelly Moser', 15, 27, 28, 140; old man's beard, 17; C. 'Perle d'Azur', 84, 105, 123; C. *rehderiana*, 93, 114; C. 'Royal Velours', 83; C. *tangutica*, 97; C. *tibetana vernayi* ('orientalis'), 32, 114; C. 'Victoria', 122; C. 'Ville de Lyon', 98; C. *viticella*, 123; C. *v.* hybrids, 132; C. *v.* 'Rubra', 32
clivia, 115
cobaea, 55
comfrey, 112
Commelina tuberosa (C. *coelestis*), 37
Convolvulus althaeoides tenuissimus, 125; C. *cneorum*, 32, 42, 105; C. *sabatius* (*mauritanicus*), 125
corn cockle, 15, 16, 17
cornflower, 15, 16, 17
Cornus, 76, 133; C. *alba* 'Elegantissima', 23, 25, 75, 124; C. *a.* 'Spaethii', 31, 75; C. *alternifolia* 'Argentea', 94; C. *canadensis*, 124; C. *mas*, 93, 114; C. *nuttallii*, 44, 144
coronilla, 97
corydalis, 138
cosmos, 105
Cotinus coggygria, 25, 27, 41, 75, 144; C. *c.* 'Foliis Purpureis', 124
Cotoneaster, 87, 114, 145; C. *salicifolius*, cowslip, 16
crab, 50
Crambe, 25; C. *cordifolia*, 28, 61, 97, 100, 144
cranesbill, 25
Crinum, 98, 134; C. x *powellii* 'Album', 143
Crocosmia, 44; C. *paniculata* (*Curtonus, Antholyza p.*), 108
Crocus, 15, 20, 44, 49, 81, 107, 108, 117; autumn c., 28; C. *imperati*, 127
x *Cupressocyparis leylandii*, 43, 60
Cupressus arizonica, 111; C. *macrocarpa* 'Goldcrest', 112
currant, 26; black c., 108; white c., 108
Cyclamen, 28, 32, 44, 69, 108, 121; C. *cilicium*, 81; C. *coum*, 81; C. *hederifolium*, 81
cypress, 54; Lawson c., 111, 127, 129; Leyland c., 43, 101; swamp c., 21, 40
Cytisus battandieri, 83, 96

daffodil, 19, 20, 26, 39, 54, 73, 108, 140, 144; d. 'Mount Hood', 108
daisy, 17; Michaelmas d., 26, 67, 73, 102, 104, 107, 138; moon d., 14
Daphne, 36, 67, 68, 112, 143; D. x *burkwoodi* 'Somerset', 67; D. *cneorum*, 67; D. *c.* 'Variegata', 67; D. *collina*, 67; D. *genkwa*, 67; D. x *neapolitana*, 67; D. *odora*, 56, 143; D. *pontica*, 67
datura, 97

Davidia involucrata, 36, 47, 54, 57, 94, 108
day lily, 107
delphinium, 25, 28, 38, 44, 49, 90, 91, 94, 98, 103, 107, 132, 138, 144
Deutzia, 135; D. *scabra*, 129
dianthus, 33, 36, 125
diascia, 33
Dicentra, 32, 73; D. *spectabilis*, 60, 83
dierama, 114
Digitalis grandiflora (*ambigua*), 110, 132; D. *lutea*, 132; D. x *mertonensis*, 110; D. *purpurea alba*, 79; D. *purpurea* 'Excelsior', 73
dog's tooth violet, 44
dogwood, 26
dove tree, 47, 108

eccremocarpus, 50
Echinops ritro, 107
Elaeagnus, 20; E. *commutata*, 32; E. x *ebbingei*, 124; E. *pungens* 'Maculata', 67
elder, golden, 124; golden cut-leaved e., 88, 89; purple leaved e., 108
elm, 46, 143; golden e., 50, 124
Elodea canadensis, 22
Enkianthus campanulatus, 108
epimedium, 36, 37
Eremurus, 60, 61; E. *robustus*, 44, 103; E. *stenophyllus* (*bungei*), 44
erigeron, 40
erodium, 125
Eryngium, 36, 102; E. *bourgatii*, 124
Erysimum 'Bowles' Mauve', 32; E. *linifolium*, 98
Erythrina crista-galli, 93
Erythronium, 109; E. *revolutum* 'White Beauty', 129; E. *tuolumnense*, 129
Escallonia, 32; E. 'Iveyi', 32
eucalyptus, 111, 112, 112, 114, 115
Eucryphia, 56, 64, 133; E. x *nymansensis*, 73; E. x *n.* 'Nymansay', 64
Euonymus alata, 26; E. *fortunei* 'Emerald 'n' Gold', 113; E. *f.* 'Silver Queen', 74; E. *japonicus*, variegated, 114
Eupatorium purpureum, 49
Euphorbia, 33, 36, 141, 144; E. *amygdaloides robbiae*, 113; E. *characias wulfenii*, 60, 98, 108; E. *cyparissias*, 82; E. *griffithii*, 44; E. *g.* 'Fireglow', 50; E. *myrsinites*, 143; E. *polychroma*, 107
Exochorda x *macrantha* 'The Bride', 97

Fabiana imbricata, 98
Fagus sylvatica, 78; F. *s. purpurea*, 78
Fatshedera lizei, 124
Fatsia japonica, 32, 124
feijoa, 112, 114
fern, 22, 115, 118, 124
feverfew, 113; golden f., 110
fig, 26, 121
Filipendula ulmaria 'Aurea', 89
fir, Greek, 48, 49, 50
flannel flower, 17
flax, perennial, 17
forget-me-not, 20, 49
foxglove, 25, 77, 105, 118, 138
freesia, 39
Fremontodendron, 97, 139; F. *californicum*, 133, 145, 146
Fritillaria (fritillary), 17, 28, 44, 69, 69; F. *acmopetala*, 105; F. *meleagris*, 105; F. *pontica*, 105

Fuchsia, 22, 37, 51, 68, 115, 118; F. 'Thalia', 98
fumitory, yellow, 49

Galanthus corcyrensis, 93; G. *nivalis* 'Miss Hasell', 48
Galtonica candicans, 105; G. *princeps*, 105
garlic, wild, 78
Garrya elliptica, 114
gean, 54
gentian, 17; willow g., 24
Geranium, 32, 55, 61, 88, 115, 132, 133; G. 'Ballerina', 97; G. *clarkei* 'Kashmir White', 98; G. *endressii*, 94; G. *e.* 'Wargrave Pink', 101; G. *ibericum*, 33, 121; G. 'Johnson's Blue', 61, 74, 97; G. *macrorrhizum*, 32; G. x *magnificum*, 107; G. *phaeum*, 32; G. *pratense album*, 98; G. *psilostemon*, 29, 90, 107; G. *sanguineum lancastriense*, 97; G. *wallichianum* 'Buxton's Variety', 20; white g., 45
geranium (pelargonium), 118, 146; scented g., 73
Gladiolus byzantinus, 41; G. *callianthus* (*Acidanthera murielae*), 105
Gleditsia, 44, 99; G. *triacanthos* 'Sunburst', 81
Gloriosa rothschildiana, 17
goat's rue, 25
golden rod, 67
gooseberry, 11, 105, 108
grass, Bowles' golden, 60; dwarf g., 125; pampas g., 19, 21; quaking g., 17
Griselinia littoralis, 40
guava, 115
guelder rose, 44
Gunnera, 22, 26, 61; G. *manicata* 73, 76, 78, 109, 109

haberlea, 124
halesia, 64
Hamamelis mollis, 140; H. 'Pallida', 60
handkerchief tree, 94
hazel, 106
Hebe, 32, 33, 56, 115, 112; H. *pinguifolia* 'Pagei', 103; H. *rakaiensis*, 76
Hedera, 118; H. *canariensis*, 143; H. *colchica* 'Dentata Varigata'; H. *helix* 'Glacier', 120; H. *h.* 'Goldheart', 49; H. 'Sulphur Heart' ('Paddy's Pride'), 49
helianthemum, 83, 146
Helichrysum, 32, 115; H. *petiolatum*, 73, 118
heliotrope, 71
Helleborus (hellebore), 32, 36, 108, 111, 114, 138; H. *corsicus*, 32, 111; H. *foetidus*, 111; H. *kochii*, 32; H. *niger* 'Potter's Wheel', 32; H. *orientalis*, 32; H. x *sternii*, 32; H. x s. 'Boughton Seedling', 37
Hemerocallis, 107, 132; H. *middendorfiana*, 107; H. 'Tejas', 107
hepatica, 32
Heracleum mantegazzianum, 61, 73
herbertia, 115
herbs, 47, 51, 110
hogweed, giant, 112
Hoheria lyallii, 98
holly, 19, 46, 47, 82, 108, 128, 131; variegated h., 50, 114
hollyhock, 138
honesty, 41
honeysuckle, 26, 44, 73, 77, 83, 84, 87, 88,

honeysuckle *Cont.*
98, *98*, 99, 112, 143; early Dutch h., 24
hop, golden, 82, 89, 124, *125*
hornbeam, 104, 114
horse chestnut, Indian, 73
Hosta, 22, 23, 36, 48, 68, 73, 76, 82, 83, 105; *H. fortunei* 'Albopicta', 107; *H.* 'Halcyon', 107; *H. plantaginea*, 114; *H. sieboldiana*, 105; *H. s.* 'Elegans', *112*; *H. sieboldii*, 21; *H. tokudama*, 124
hoya, 17
Humulus lupulus aureus, 82, 84, 89, 97
hyacinth, 115; grape h., 13, 28
Hydrangea, 22, 118, 146; *H. aspera villosa*, 84; lacecap h., 76; *H.* 'Lanarth White', *125*; *H. paniculata* 'Grandiflora', 83, 84; *H. p.* 'Praecox', 83; *H. petiolaris*, 56, 84, 87, 146

Ilex x altaclerensis 'Golden King', 83, 84
ilex oak, 145
incarvillea, 60
Indigofera heterantha (*gerardiana*), 99; *I. potaninii*, 99
Ipomoea, 17; *I.* 'Heavenly Blue', 15
Iris, 32, 69, 73, *112*, 138, 140; *I. foetidissima*, 60; *I. innominata*, 107; *I. pallida* 'Variegata', 105, *112*; *I. reticulata*, 28; *I. sibirica*, 79, 109; *I. unguicularis* (*stylosa*), 28; variegated i., 92
Itea ilicifolia, 109
ivy, *12*, 17, 26; variegated i., 84, 87, *125*

Jasminum (jasmine), 44, 49, 98, 115, 143; *J. officinale*, 73, 79, 98; *J. revolutum*, 37; *J. x stephanense*, 97
Judas tree, 92
Juniperus (juniper), 45, 50, 132; *J. communis* 'Hibernica', 37; *J.* 'Skyrocket', 98; *J. virginiana* 'Grey Owl', 77

kaffir lily, 114
kalmia, 118
Kniphofia, 40; *K. caulescens*, 114
Koelreuteria paniculata, 97
Kolkwitzia amabilis, 31

laburnum, 17, 26, 73
Lamium 'Beacon Silver', 84
Laurus nobilis, *120*
laurustinus, 20
Lavandula (lavender), 32, 61, 92, 99, *110*, 139; 'Hidcote' l., 86, 132; 'Munstead' l., *134*; old English l., 138
lavatera, 105
lent lily, 73
lettuce 'Little Gem', *108*; l. 'Tom Thumb', *108*
leucojum, 108
Ligularia dentata 'Desdemona', 21, 50, 68; *L. d.* 'Othello', 68; *L. macrophylla*, 50; *L. przewalskii*, 50, 68; *L. p.* 'The Rocket', 109, *112*
lilac, 17, 31, 36, 37, 46, 50, 138
Lilium (lily), 25, 26, 32, 43, *51*, 58, 60, 77, 79, 88, 107, 146; *L. auratum*, 140; *L. candidum* (Madonna l.), 35, 39, 71, 144; *L. lancifolium* (*L. tigrinum*, tiger lily), 46, 47; *L. regale*, 73, *103*, 104, 105, 111, 132, 144
lily, kaffir, 114
lime, 19, 111, *134*, 143; pleached l., 44, 76, 104

liquidambar, 73, 76, 114
Liriodendron tulipifera, 46, 47, *112*
Lithospermum 'Heavenly Blue', 42
Lobelia, 30, 118; *L. cardinalis*, 132
Lonicera x brownii 'Fuchsioides', 97; *L. japonica*, 77; *L. nitida*, 19, 22, 108; *L. n.* 'Baggesen's Gold', *110*, 124; *L. periclymenum*, 77; *L. p.* 'Serotina', 98; *L. tragophylla*, 98
love-in-a-mist, 107
lupin, 98, 138, 139, 144
Lychnis, 94; *L. chalcedonica*, 107; *L. coronaria alba*, 90
Lysichiton americanum, 26, 109
Lysimachia punctata, 38

Macleaya cordata, 50
Magnolia, 26, 36, 37, 47, 54, 56, 64, *112*, 116; *M. grandiflora*, 56, 133, 145; *M. g.* 'Exmouth', 97; *M. hypoleuca* (*obovata*), 133; *M. kobus*, 19; *M. kobus loebneri* 'Leonard Messel', 36; *M. salicifolia*, 54; *M. x soulangiana*, 29, 93, 113, 139, 144; *M. wilsonii*, 47, 133
Mahonia, 55, 64; *M.* 'Charity', 60; *M. japonica*, 60
mallow, 71
Maltese cross flower, 107
Malus, 123; *M. floribunda*, 61; *M.* 'John Downie', 104
maple, field m., *112*; Japanese m., 47; snakebark m., 102
marigold, corn, 17; marsh m., 68, *106*, 109
marjoram, golden, *51*, 132
marrubium, 33
May tree, 53
Meconopsis grandis, 108; *M. g.* G. S. 600, 50
medlar, *12*, 59
Melissa officinalis 'Aurea', *103*
Mentha rotundifolia, 73
Menyanthes trifoliata, 109
Metasequoia glyptostroboides, 19, 36, 40, 59, 73, 76, *106*
mimulus, 69
monkshood, 49
mulberry, 26, 59
muscari, *58*
myrtle, *112*, 115, 146

Nandina domestica, 93
Narcissus, 13, 19, 36, 44, 50, 73, 101, 103, 107, 108; *N.* 'Beersheba', 81; *N.* 'Mount Hood', 81; Poeticus n., 81
nectarine, 16
Nepeta, 92, 104, *120*; *N.* 'Six Hills Giant', *121*
nerine, 98
Nicotiana, 71; *N. sylvestris*, *58*
Nothofagus fusca, 133
nut, 111

oak, 19, 127, 128; evergreen o., 111; Turkey o., 75
old man's beard, 17
Olearia macrodonta, 31; *O. x scilloniensis*, 33, 98
omphalodes, 32
orchid, 73
origanum, 101, *125*
Osmanthus x burkwoodii, 31; *O. delavayi*, 76; *O. heterophyllus*, 76
osteospermum, 33

oxalis, 17
ozothamnus, 33

Paeonia (peony), 20, 25, 26, 27, 32, 36, 60, 73, 85, 88, 89, 102, 144; *P. mlokosewitschii*, 44; *P.* 'Sarah Bernhardt', 27; tree p., 44, 72
pansy, 20, 43, 49
Papaver somniferum, 40, *41*
parahebe, 101
Parrotia persica, 114
Parthenocissus quinquefolia, 26
passiflora, 115
paulownia, *58*, 60, 99
pea, sweet, 17, 26, 50, 55, 79, p. 'Hurst Green Shaft', *108*
pear, 99, 46; espalier p., 105; weeping silver p., 72, 99
Pelargonium, 30, 39; *P.* 'Duchess of Eastbourne', 86
peltiphyllum, 22, 61, 79
Penstemon, 32, 71, 114, 138; *P.* 'Charles Rudd', 109; *P. glaber*, 109; *P.* 'Heavenly Blue', 132
periploca, 114
periwinkle, 46, 47
Perovskia atriplicifolia, 32
Petasites, 61, 79; *P. japonicus giganteus*, 76
petunia, 26, 43, 146
Philadelphus, 31, 44, 61, 77, 88, 132, 133, 140; *P.* 'Belle Etoile', 84; *P. coronarius* 'Aureus', 83, 109; *P. microphyllus*, 132
phlomis, 38
Phlox, 39, 73, 114; alpine p., 87, 146; *P. maculata* 'Alpha', 124; *P. m.* 'Omega', *125*; *P. paniculata*, 44
Phormium, 61, 91, *112*, 115; *P. tenax* 'Variegatum', *115*
Physostegia virginiana 'Vivid', 107, *108*
Picea breweriana, 109
Pieris, 64; *P. formosa forrestii*, 56
pink, 25, 31, *58*, 60, 73, *133*, 139
Pinus (pine); *P. bungeana*, *58*, 60; Scots p., 19, 21, 22; umbrella p., 133
piptanthus, 82
Pittosporum, 64, 111; *P. tenuifolium*, 132
plumbago, 115
polemonium, 83
polyanthus, 13, 69
Polygonum affine 'Darjeeling Red', *120*, *121*
pomegranate, 112
poplar, 59, 108; balsam p., 43, 133
poppy, *16*, 17, 39, 138; Himalayan p., 50; opium p., 40, *41*; oriental p., 40, 44, 107; o.p. 'Black and White', 89; p. 'Pink Chiffon', 107; Welsh p., 13
Populus balsamifera, 79; *P. candicans* 'Aurora', 76; *P. lasiocarpa*, 99
Potentilla, 88, 132, 144; *P.* 'Elizabeth', 98
primrose, 22, 73, 109, 138
Primula, 21, 22, 26, 28, 44, 45, 64, 68, 69, 108, 109, 117, 124, 138, 144; *P. auricula*, 84, 105; *P.* 'Bartley Strain', *106*; Candelabra p., 108, *112*; *P.* 'Postford White', 109; *P. pulverulenta*, *106*, 109; *P. sibthorpii*, 107
Prunus, 20, 82, 99; *P. cerasifera* 'Pissardii', 124; *P. x cistena*, 123, 124; *P.* 'Sekiyama' (*P.* 'Kanzan'), 29; *P. serrula*, 36, 43; *P. serrulata*, 43; *P. subhirtella* 'Autumnalis', 81, 140; *P. s.* 'A. Rosea', 36; *P.* 'Tai Haku', 32; *P.* 'Ukon', 32, 140; *P. virginiana*

Prunus Cont.
'Shubert', 99
Ptelea trifoliata 'Aurea', 77
Pulmonaria, 32, 37; *P. rubra* 'Redstart', 107
Pulsatilla vulgaris, 109
pyrethrum, 139
Pyrus calleryana 'Chanticleer', *102, 104*; *P. salicifolia* 'Pendula', 54, 72, 73, 83, 98, 105, 114

quince, 59; Japanese q., 17

ramonda, 124
raspberry, 26, 108
redwood, dawn, *106*
Rhamnus alaternus 'Argenteovariegata', 114
Rheum, 108; *R. palmatum*, 41; *R. p.* 'Atrosanguineum', 73, 79; *R. p.* 'Bowles' Crimson', *113*
Rhododendron, 19, 53, 54, 55, 56, 63, 64, 64, 108, 118, 128, *135*; *R. augustinii*, 54; *R. dauricum*, 127; *R.* Elizabeth, 54; *R.* 'Fragrantissimum', 44, 79; *R.* 'John', 64; *R.* 'Julian Williams', 64; *R.* 'Lady Alice Fitzwilliam', 129; *R.* 'Lawrence', 64; *R.* 'Philip', 64; *R. ponticum*, 56, 118; *R. protistum* var. *giganteum*, 127, 129; *R. tephropeplum*, *129*
rhubarb, 61
rhus, 61
Ribes odoratum, 99
Robinia pseudacacia 'Frisia', 94, 98, 112, 124; *R. p.* 'Inermis', 104
rock rose, 87
Rodgersia, 22, 61; *R. podophylla*, 108
Romneya coulteri, 37, 44
Rosa (rose), 17, 26, 27, 44, 49, 75, 79, 81, 87, 89, 98, 105, 112, 115, 117, 120, 123, 131, 133, 138, 144, 145; *R.* 'Admiral Rodney', 16; *R.* 'Alain', 71; Alba r., 101; *R. alba* 'Great Maiden's Blush', 66; *R.* 'Alba Semiplena', 61; *R.* 'Albertine', 49, 61, 120; *R.* 'Alchemist', 84; *R.* 'Aloha', 124; *R.* 'Anna', 99; *R.* 'Ballerina', 55; Banksian r., 145; *R.* 'Blairii No. II', 49; *R.* 'Blanc Double de Coubert', *103*, 105, 132; *R.* 'Bleu Magenta', *113*; *R.* 'Bloomfield Abundance', 124; *R.* 'Blue Moon', 16; *R.* 'Bobbie James', 81; Bourbon r., 101; *R.* 'Brenda Colvin', 92; *R.* 'Buff Beauty', 25, 31, 55, 120, 132; *R. californica* 'Plena', 81; *R.* 'Camaieux', *146*; *R.* 'Canary Bird', 60, *138, 139*; *R.* 'Cardinal de Richelieu', 27, 132; *R.* 'Céleste', 37, 50, *58*, 83; *R.* 'Cerise Bouquet', 61; *R.* 'Chapeau de Napoléon', 132; *R.* 'Chaplin's Pink Climber', 71; *R.* 'Charles de Mills', 27, 81; China r., 47, 49, 114; *R.* 'Chinatown', 61; *R. chinensis*, 114; *R. chinensis* 'Mutabilis', 32; *R.* 'Climbing Cécile Brunner', 37; *R.* 'Climbing Iceberg', 83, *104*; *R.* 'Complicata', 33, 61, *132, 133*; *R.* 'Constance Spry', 26, 27, 71, 82, 94, *116*, 120, 132, *133*; *R.* 'Cornelia', 25, 29, 55, 97, 120; Damask r., 50; dog r., 16; *R.* 'Dorothy Perkins', 49; *R.* 'Ednaston Climber', 99; *R. elegantula* 'Persetosa' (*R. farreri Persetosa*), 60; *R.* 'Elmshorn', 124; *R.* 'Emily Gray', 49; *R.* 'Étoile de Hollande', 16; *R.* 'Fantin Latour', *85*, 131, *146*; *R.* 'Felicia', 25, 29, 55, 71, *146*; *R.* 'Félicité Parmentier', *135*; *R. filipes*, 50; *R.*

'Flora McIver', 140; Floribunda r., 55; *R.* 'Francis E. Lester', 76; *R.* 'François Juranville', 143; *R.* 'Frau Dagmar Hastropp', 74, 143; *R.* 'Fritz Nobis', 55, 81, *134*, 141; Gallica r., 50, 101; *R.* 'George Dickson', 26; *R. glauca* (*rubrifolia*), 25, 36, 83, 91, 94, *102*, 118, *132, 135*; *R.* 'Gloire de Dijon', 84; *R.* 'Goldbusch', *116*; *R.* 'Golden Dawn', 16; *R.* 'Golden Showers', 83; *R.* 'Golden Wings', 61; *R.* 'Gypsy Boy', *133*; *R.* 'Henri Martin', *132*; *R.* 'Honorine de Brabant', 83; *R. hugonis*, 50; Hybrid Musk r., 25, 29, 54, 76, 120; Hybrid Tea r., 22, 101, 143; *R.* 'Iceberg', 14, 59, 61, 84, *140*; *R.* 'Ispahan', 44, 50, 83; *R.* 'Kazanlik', *146*; *R.* 'Kiftsgate', 92; *R.* 'Koenigin von Dänemarck', 83, 131; *R.* 'Lavender Lassie', 71, 91; *R.* 'La Ville de Bruxelles', 50; *R. longicuspis*, 60; *R.* 'Mme Alfred Carrière', *104, 130*; *R.* 'Mme Caroline Testout', 84; *R.* 'Mme Grégoire Staechelin', 84, 88; *R.* 'Mme Isaac Pereire', 101, *113*; *R.* 'Mme Lauriol de Barny', *51*; *R.* 'Mme Plantier', 61; *R.* 'Magenta', 71; *R.* 'Maigold', 60, 131; *R.* 'Maréchal Niel', 16; *R.* 'Margaret Merril', 139; *R.* 'Marguerite Hilling', 89; *R.* 'Mermaid', 93; moss r., 88; *R. moyesii*, 114; *R. m.* 'Geranium', 81; *R.* 'Moyesii Superba', 57; musk r., 88; *R.* 'Natalie Nypels', *58*; *R.* 'Nevada', 33, 57, 60, 131, *140*; *R.* 'New Dawn', 12, 32, 49, 98; *R.* 'Norwich Pink', 88; *R.* 'Paulii', 49, 88; *R.* 'Paul's Himalayan Musk', 65, *146*; *R.* 'Paul's Scarlet Climber', 49; *R.* 'Pax', 120, *121*; *R.* 'Penelope', 25, 29, 37, 71, 76, 97, 120, *146*; *R.* 'Petite de Hollande', 83; *R.* 'Pink Grootendorst', 37; *R.* 'Pinkie', 99; *R.* 'Pink Pearl', 84; *R.* 'Pompon de Paris', 94; Poulsen r., 25; *R.* 'Prelude', 71; *R. primula*, 97; *R.* 'Prosperity', 55, 71, 76; *R.* 'Queen Elizabeth', 61, 143; *R.* 'Radox Bouquet', 139; *R.* 'Rambling Rector', 27, 28, 76, 92; *R.* 'Raubritter', 58; *R.* 'Reine des Violettes', 98; *R. richardii* (*sancta*), 61; Rosa Mundi, 101; *R.* 'Rose de Resht', 83; Rugosa r., 73, 88, 114, 120; *R.* 'Sanders' White Rambler', 19, 133; *R.* 'Scabrosa', 110; *R.* 'Seagull', 61, 76; shrub r., 32, 43, 69, 72, 73, 83, 91, 109, 112, *144*; *R.* 'Spek's Yellow', 27; *R.* 'Stirling Silver', 16; *R.* 'Texas Centennial', 143; *R.* 'The Fairy', 83, 93; *R.* 'Thisbe', *132*; *R.* 'Tricolore de Flandre', 27; *R.* 'Tuscany', *132*; 'Tuscany Superb', *132*; *R.* 'Uncle Walter', 90; *R.* 'Veilchenblau', 81; *R.* 'Violette', 97; *R. webbiana*, 77; *R.* 'Wedding Day', 27, 28, 114, *132*; *R.* 'William Allen Richardson', 16; *R.* 'William Lobb', 83, 97; *R. willmottiae*, 60; *R. xanthina* 'Canary Bird', 114; *R.* 'Zéphirine Drouhin', 27, 105
Rosmarinus (rosemary), 32, 33; Corsican r., *146*; *R. officinalis*, *138*
Rubus Tridel, *146*; *R. T.* 'Beneden', 50
rudbeckia, 49
Ruta (rue), 25, 61, *133*; *R. graveolens* 'Jackman's Blue', 83, *120*

sage, Afghan, 32
Salix, 76; *S. alba argentea* (*S. a. sericea*), 59, 78; *S. exigua*, 59; *S. fargesii*, *135*
Salvia, 36; *S. aurea*, *110*; *S. farinacea*, *132*; *S.*

involucrata 'Bethellii', *107*; *S. leucantha*, 109; *S. officinalis* 'Tricolor', 105; *S. patens*, 132, 143; *S. sclarea turkestanica*, 110; *S. x superba*, 40; *S. uliginosa*, 132
Sambucus nigra 'Marginata', *114*
Sanguinaria canadensis, 98
Santolina, 32, 33, 61, 71, 105, 132; *S. chamaecyparissus*, 20
scabious, 111
scilla, 20, 81, 83, 140
Sedum 'Autumn Joy', 25, 38, 40, *108*; *S. spectabile*, 25, 29, 143
Senecio, 32, 61, 71; *S. italicus*, 97; *S.* 'Sunshine', 75
Sisyrinchium, 29; *S. striatum* 'Aunt May', 105
snowdrop, 15, 20, 28, 32, 46, 47, 48, 60, 69, 69, 73, 81, 93, 107, 139, 140
Solanum, 112; *S. jasminoides*, 98; *S. j* 'Album', 93
solidago, *108*
solidaster, 107
sollya, 114
Solomon's seal, 73
sophora, 60
Sorbus, 99; *S. hupehensis*, 98, 98; *S.* 'Joseph Rock', 98, 98
southernwood, *51*, 143
sphaeralcea, 125
spinach, mountain, red, 25
spindle, 44
spruce, Colorado white, 114; Sitka s., 64
Stachys macrantha, 107; *S. olympica*, 83
star of Bethlehem, 50
Stephanandra incisa, 26
Stewartia malacodendron, *133*; *S. pseudocamellia*, 133
stock, 73, 79; night scented s., 28, 73
strawberry, 108
sweet pea, 17, 26, 50, 55, 79; perennial s. p., 98
sweet rocket, *100*
sycamore, 142
Syringa, 132; *S. x josiflexa* 'Bellicent', 37; *S. x persica*, 31

Taxodium, 59; *T. distichum*, 19, 21
Taxus baccata, 75
tecoma, 112
Teucrium fruticans, 31, 73, 105
thalictrum, 25
thistle, Scotch, 13, 41
thorn, *103*
Thuja, hedge, 111; *T. plicata*, 75
Thujopsis dolabrata, 129
Thymus (thyme), 32, 33, 83, 139, 146
tibouchina, 115
Trachelospermum jasminoides, 98
Tricyrtis stolonifera, 105
Trillium, 124; *T. sessile*, 109
trollius, 108
Tulipa (tulip), 13, 20, 20, 25, 28, 43, 45, *51*, 58, 83, 97, 141; *T.* 'Apricot Beauty', 25; *T.* 'China Pink', 61; *T.* 'Niphetos', 24; *T.* 'Queen of Bartigons', 24; *T.* 'Sorbet', 24; *T. tarda*, 32; *T.* 'The Bishop', 24; *T. urumiensis*, 32; *T.* 'White Triumphator', 60
tulip tree, 46

Valerian, wild, 14, 25
Verbascum bombyciferum, 110, 119; *V. olympicum*, 60

Veronica incana, 132
Viburnum, 31, 36, 64, 79, 114, 132; *V. x
bodnantense* 'Dawn', 32; *V. x b.* 'Deben',
97; *V. x burkwoodii*, 124; *V. carlesii*, 84;
V. davidii, 92; *V. farreri*, 32, 50; *V. opulus*
'Xanthocarpum', 81; *V.* 'Park Farm', 60,
109; *V. plicatum*, 72, 115; *V. p.* 'Lanarth',
36, 59, 114; *V. p.* 'Mariesii', 36, 79, 81, 88
vine, 26, 87, 88
Viola, 32, 36; *V. cornuta*, 51; *V. c. alba*, 83
violet, 17, 39, 108, 138; Parma v., 50
violet, dog's tooth, 44

Virginia creeper, 17, 26, 49, 61
Vitis 'Brant', 49, 73; *V. coignetiae*, 84, 120,
121, 124

wallflower, 20
walnut, 59
waterlily, 17, 54, 56, 111, 112, 145, 146
Wattakaka sinensis, 93
Weigela, 64, 88; *W. florida* 'Foliis Purpureis',
89; *W.* 'Variegata', 25
Wellingtonia, 59
willow, 17, 19, 40; weeping w., 109

winter sweet, 114, 127
Wisteria, 17, 28, 44, 50, 71, 73, 84, 92, 99,
99, 112, 130, 133, 145, 145; *W. venusta*, 73
witch hazel, 114, 127
wood sorrel, 129

yew, 45, 47, 51, 59, 76, 83, 87, 88, 92, 118,
119, 120; golden y., 35, 57, 143; y. hedge,
18, 19, 20, 26, 44, 60, 88, 91, 98, 101,
102, 104, 118, 143
Yorkshire fog, 17
Yucca, 91; *Y. filamentosa*, 79